DATE DUE			

THE BEST OF FINNISH COOKING

Taimi Previdi

HIPPOCRENE BOOKS
New York

To Robert, Bob and Jeffrey, whose enjoyment of Finnish cooking made this book possible

For information, address:
HIPPOCRENE BOOKS, INC.
171 Madison Avenue
New York, NY 10016

Library of Congress Cataloging-in-Publication Data

Previdi, Taimi
The best of Finnish cooking / Taimi Previdi.
p. cm.
Includes index.
ISBN 0-7818-0284-9 : $19.95
1. Cookery, Finnish. I. Title.
TX723.5.F5P74 1994
641.594897—dc20 94-40852
CIP

Printed in the United States of America.

CONTENTS

FOREWORD

This book was originally compiled for my two American-born sons who wanted to have recipes for the Finnish foods I frequently cooked, but who could not read the recipes in Finnish. The book is designed for all those who want to experience the fresh, savory taste of Finnish cooking, especially for those of Finnish descent who wish to preserve this delightful part of their heritage, the distinctive flavor of Finnish cooking.

These recipes have been collected over the years from various sources in Finland; some I have inherited from my mother and my family, some from friends, some from various Finnish publications and books. I have modified most of the recipes somewhat and adapted all to the American kitchen; some Finnish ingredients are difficult to find in the United States, some ingredients do not have the same flavor as their Finnish equivalents, and of course, the measurements are different. Nevertheless, I have done my best to keep the recipes as close as possible to the Finnish originals, so that the foods taste the way I remember them growing up in Finland.

There are often many different delicious variations of Finnish dishes and I have tried to pick the tastiest ones. I have also tried to include recipes from all regions of the land, to make this a representative sample of Finnish foods. The greatest challenge I faced was recapturing the special taste of foods eaten in Finland.

I hope that these recipes enable people of Finnish descent, as well as people who have visited Finland and adventuresome cooks everywhere, to cook the way Finns do every day.

Introduction and Cooking Tips

Finland is a country with thousands of lakes and deep forests. Its northern location makes winters long and summers short. The growing season is also short, and accordingly, when fresh produce, vegetables and fruits are in season, they are prized and served in abundance. Almost every household does some preserving for winter, be it homemade strawberry jam or pickled cucumbers. Most households have freezers where they can store produce from their own garden. Even suburban homeowners often have a small garden plot tucked away in their yard growing tomatoes, carrots, lettuce, and herbs. Apple trees in the yards are very popular. So are gooseberry bushes and blackcurrant bushes.

In the old days almost all houses had cellars where potatoes, cabbages, carrots and the like were stored for the whole winter. During really cold days, before farmhouses had electricity, a bucket of hot embers was taken to the cellar to keep the produce from freezing. Modern day Finland, of course, has all the conveniences, including greenhouses, from which fresh produce is available all year.

Much traditional Finnish cooking relies on the seasons. In winter soups, stews and casseroles are prepared, while in summertime fresh fruits and vegetables are served with as little cooking as possible. Finns take advantage of the fresh harvest of the brief summer.

As Finland was part of Sweden for hundreds of years, Finnish cooking has been influenced by Swedish traditions. Finland was also part of Russia for over a hundred years, and Russian influence shows itself in some Finnish dishes. Mainly, Finnish cooking is simple, flavorful and not spicy, relying heavily on the natural flavor of foods. In Finland it is said that in preparing dishes only ingredients that make a strong contribution to the taste of the food should be added.

Favorite Foods

Potatoes. Potatoes have always been the mainstay of Finnish cooking, and they are served as a side dish with almost every meal. Many casseroles and soups also have potatoes as the main ingredient with meat and vegetables used only as flavorings.

Bread. Bread is another Finnish specialty, and baking homemade bread is still very popular. Most Finnish breads are made with whole grains: rye, oats, wheat and barley. Sourdough Finnish rye bread is what many expatriate Finns miss the most and ask for when they come back for a visit.

Coffee Breads and Cakes. Finns are champion coffee drinkers and naturally coffee must always be accompanied by cakes and cookies, especially *pulla*, the famous Finnish coffee braid. It is still a well-known tradition that if you are giving a coffee party, you must serve at least seven different kinds of cookies and cakes.

Fish. Finland's lakes and Baltic waters have always been an excellent source of fish, even in winter, when the lakes and coastlines freeze over. Ice fishing is popular in Finland, and countless are the fishermen, who still chop a hole in the ice and sit in the freezing temperatures trying to catch something. Many of the fish caught in Finland are not available America, especially the Baltic herring, *silakka*, that is eaten boiled, salted, fried, baked, smoked, pickled, grilled and casseroled.

Berries. Finnish forests provide a wide variety of berries. It is a common day trip in the fall, even for schoolchildren, to take a basket and head to the nearest woods for an abundance of blueberries, lingonberries, and cranberries. Home gardens and marketplaces provide gooseberries, blackcurrants and red currants. The berries that do not get eaten right away are made into pies or sweet soups and jams. Finland also grows two berries that are made into flavorful liqueurs: cloudberry, *lakka* or *suomuurain*, and arctic brambleberry, *mesimarja*.

Mushrooms. Picking wild mushrooms is also a popular day trip for Finns. Mushroom and berry picking is also encouraged by the common law that allows mushroom and berry picking on private lands, as long as it is not done close to buildings and yards and does not create a nuisance for the owner. Mushrooms that are not immediately cooked are salted, pickled or frozen for future use.

Here are a few items that should always be available in a well-stocked Finnish kitchen:

Salt. Finns used to salt their food rather heavily, due to use of salt as a preservative. Recently, as people have become more conscious of healthy eating habits, the use of salt as seasoning has declined. These recipes use a modest amount of salt, which can always be increased during or after cooking, according to individual tastes. Coarse salt or kosher salt is used for salting fish and preserves, but it can be replaced by common table salt.

Allspice, whole or ground, is used extensively in Finnish cooking, often replacing black pepper, and often, as in Finnish meatballs, it provides the characteristic Finnish taste. The flavor of allspice is a mixture of cloves, nutmeg, cinnamon and juniper berries.

White Pepper, whole or ground, is used instead of black pepper in flavoring Finnish meats and fish. White pepper comes from the same plant as black pepper, being the fully matured berry with the covering removed. It is slightly more pungent than black pepper, but black pepper can always be substituted for white pepper in the recipes. The only dishes where white pepper is more desirable are light-colored dishes, such as fish dishes and light sauces, where you might not want to see the black specks of pepper.

Cardamom. This spice is indispensable in Finnish baking, as the sweet yeast coffee breads get their distinctive flavor from the spice.

Bay Leaves. This herb is used in Finnish soups and stews, and also often to flavor fish broths and pickles. Only fresh dried, preferably imported, bay leaves should be used.

Dill is the most extensively used herb in Finland. When the first dill sprigs appear in the spring in home gardens, they are sprinkled liberally over a wide variety of dishes, and are especially indispensable with cucumbers, new potatoes and fish. Fresh dill, which of course is now available year 'round, should be used in all recipes; the dried variety in stores does not have much flavor. You can dry your own dill by hanging small bunches upside down from a string in a warm place. Some of the dill in Finnish gardens is allowed to flower and form heads, or so-called "crowns," which contain dill seeds. They are used in pickling and in cooking crayfish.

Marjoram, a relative of oregano, is another herb that is extensively used in Finnish cooking for flavoring meats and soups. It can also be dried in bunches the same way as dill, and stored in tightly closed tins.

Parsley is another popular herb in Finland. It is not only used for garnishing dishes, but it is considered a vitamin-rich addition for a healthy diet, especially in winter, and is chopped and sprinkled liberally over sandwiches and many dishes.

Boston Lettuce. The lettuce of choice in Finland has always been Boston lettuce, which is grown in home gardens, and used not only in salads, but to decorate sandwiches and food platters. You will always find a leaf or two of Boston lettuce on Finnish dinner plates along with a couple of wedges of tomato or a few slices of cucumber, as health-conscious Finns want to eat fresh vegetables at every meal.

Cucumbers. Another vegetable much favored by Finns is the cucumber, which is served at almost every meal in the summer, either just sliced, or in a cucumber salad. The long, seedless European-type cucumber is specified in these recipes, but you can replace it with the ordinary cucumber, in which case it is preferable to peel it (as it is covered with wax), split it in half, and remove the seeds with a teaspoon.

Tomatoes. Finns also love tomatoes. They are mostly eaten fresh, and no wonder, as most of the tomatoes on the market have been allowed to vine-ripen and are soft and bursting with flavor and juice.

Vanilla Sugar and Vanillin Sugar. Finns mostly use vanillin in the form of vanillin sugar in baking, instead of vanilla extract. If you want to get the authentic vanillin taste in baked goods, some German delicatessens sell it, as do some Scandinavian stores. You can make your own vanilla sugar to use for sprinkling on baked goods by splitting a vanilla bean and burying it in a pound of powdered sugar in a tightly closed jar. Wait for a few days for the flavor to develop before using it.

Cooking Tips

Margarine. Finns often use margarine instead of butter in cooking, especially in baking.

Sauce thickening. Finns often thicken sauces and soups by mixing flour with water, rather then using the more common method of cooking the flour in butter. This method is especially good for people who want to reduce their fat intake. When thickening soups and sauces, granulated "instant" flour, such as "Wondra" is very handy, since it mixes with water very well. It is available in most supermarkets.

Dessert soups. Finnish dessert soups are sweet soups that are sometimes made thin as soup, sometimes thick as pudding, or *kiisseli*. You can easily switch between those two by adding a little bit more water or less starch to make soup out of a pudding or by adding a little bit more starch or less water to thicken a soup into a pudding. The thinner soups are often used as an accompaniment for porridges and pancakes, whereas the thicker puddings are often served with cream or whipped cream.

Potato starch. Finns use potato starch instead of cornstarch for baking and thickening puddings and fruit soups. It can be replaced with cornstarch, but a slightly larger quantity and slightly longer cooking period is required.

Cane syrup. Finns use cane syrup or beet syrup, made with sugar beets, rather than molasses or dark corn syrup in cooking and baking. If you are not able to get the Scandinavian syrup, the common pancake syrup is closer to the taste of Finnish syrup than either molasses or dark corn syrup.

Parchment paper. Parchment paper, which is commonly used in Finland, and which is available in many supermarkets, hardware stores and baking supply stores, is invaluable in baking. Parchment paper tolerates heat very well, and makes it unnecessary to grease the baking sheets. It helps in transferring delicate doughs from one place to another and in unmolding cakes. It can also be used to seal foods during baking. You can use wax paper in lining pans for baking cakes, such as jelly rolls, but for baking cookies and yeast breads, real parchment paper is required, if you want to avoid greasing pans.

Plett pan. Almost every household in Finland has one of these cast iron skillets for making pancakes. It is a pan with 4 to 7 round sections that allow you to cook several pancakes simultaneously. They are available at stores catering to Scandinavian customers (see appendix, page 228)

Since appetites and serving sizes vary, the number of servings in each dish have not been specified. The servings are intended for 4-6 people, unless otherwise stated.

FINNISH CUSTOMS AND MENUS FOR SPECIAL OCCASIONS

AN OLD-FASHIONED FINNISH COFFEE PARTY
Kahvikutsut

The Finns are among the most devoted coffee drinkers in the world. They like their coffee quite strong, and it is served from small dainty cups, similar to demitasse cups. The coffee is not black, however, it is normally roasted very light to avoid bitterness. Coffee is served for breakfast, midmorning break, lunch, afternoon coffee break, dinner and for visitors who drop by any time of day. Often friends are invited over for coffee, but of course it's not just coffee that is on the menu. First, sliced coffee bread is served, then a couple of dry cakes, then some cookies, then a filled dessert cake or small filled cakes called *leivokset* are served. For people who do not like sweets, some sugarless pastries are often provided, such as butter buns or small crackers with sliced cheese. After 2-3 cups of strong coffee and inspired discussion, some open-faced sandwiches are often served, or some other small salty snack, with tea as accompaniment. This is playfully called throwing-out tea, which means that the guests are expected to leave after the last tea has been consumed.

Here is a typical coffee party menu, with recipes provided in the appropriate sections of the cookbook:

Cardamom Coffee Braid
Buttermilk Cake
Sand Cake
Spoon Cookies
Rye Cookies
Alexander's Tarts
Strawberry Cake
Butter Buns
Open-faced Ham Sandwiches
Open-faced Cheese Sandwiches
Coffee, Tea, Milk, Mineral Water

EASTER
Pääsiäinen

In Finland, Easter has always been a very solemn festival. It is quite different from the flower-filled spring festival that it is in the United States. In March or April the ground is still covered with snow. There are no wildflowers available, but tables are decorated with pussywillows which are sometimes called palms. On Good Friday most of the stores and restaurants are closed and the mood is somber as fits the occasion. In the countryside, and especially in Karelia, Easter Saturday used to be considered an unholy day, when evil spirits reigned. Easter witches were said to be flying on their broomsticks from their homes on Kyöpeli Mountain (*Kyöpelinvuori*). Young people went from house to house with willow twigs, knocking on people's doors and waving the twigs to dispel evil spirits and bring good luck to the house. Reward consisted of some sweets for the children, not unlike Halloween in the United States.

On Easter morning, it was said, if you got up before dawn and went up a hill to see the sun rise, you could actually see the sun dancing for joy. All the evil spirits were conquered, and the world was happy once more.

There are a number of special foods in Finland eaten only at Easter. One of the dishes that is unique for Finnish Easter is *mämmi*, a malted rye porridge that is cooked on the stove a whole day and then baked in the oven for several hours. It used to be served in containers made out of birch bark, but nowadays, of course, the containers are made of cardboard with pictures of birch bark printed on them. *Mämmi* is eaten for dessert with sugar and cream. Another dish that is served only at Easter is a fresh cheese dish called *pasha*. This dish comes from Russia via Karelia, but has spread recently throughout Finland for dessert at Easter. Fresh *pulla* is baked with raisins added to the dough for the occasion. Eggs are eaten in every form, and on Easter Sunday many families serve Easter lamb, a leg of lamb, or a crown of lamb.

Here are some menu suggestions for Easter:

Sliced Smoked Ham
Deviled Eggs
Cooked Vegetable Salad
Roast Leg of Lamb
Oven Roasted Potatoes
Creamed Spinach
Old-fashioned Lettuce Salad
Wheat Loaf with Butter
***Mämmi* with Cream and Sugar**
***Pasha* with Fruits**
Viipuri Twist
Tosca Cake
Coffee, Tea, Milk, Mineral Water

MAY DAY
Vappu

In the United States there is no May Day celebration on May 1st, so it may be difficult for Americans to understand what the fuss is all about. Well, the winters in Finland are long and hard, with snow covering the ground from November to April in southern Finland, and in the northern parts even longer. In April the snow cover on the roads and sidewalks is finally melting, the sun is coaxing out the first shy spring flowers, and people feel that maybe, just maybe, there is going to be a summer after all.

That May Day was originally a pagan ritual doesn't dampen the enthusiasm with which people face the coming of May. The day is a holiday for everybody. Students who have spent the spring studying for tests, and who have finally been rewarded with a baccalaureat degree and a white cap, joyfully wear it, as do former students who fish them out from among mothballs. Labor unions parade with their flags. Outdoor restaurants open, and never mind that the temperature is sometimes quite chilly, people wear their spring finery and promenade outdoors. Children and grown-ups alike carry balloons.

On May Day Eve, young people simply have to have a date to go dancing, and often the evening turns out to be quite a celebration. That is why a special May Day lunch is served in many restaurants and homes, with emphasis on herring dishes, which are supposed to cure the inevitable hangovers.

May Day lunch in most of the restaurants consists of *seisova pöytä*, which means smorgasbord, or buffet. Cold fish and meats are accompanied by salads, a couple of hot dishes, cheeses, breads and desserts. And of course on May Day, everybody drinks *sima*, a sparkling lemon drink rather like mead, often homemade. To accompany sima May Day crullers or *tippaleivät*, delicate doughnuts, are served, specially made for the day.

Some sample dishes for a smorgasbord follow. Recipes for all prepared dishes are included in this book. Of course, not all of the following dishes need to be included in a smorgasbord. The custom is to include one or two dishes from each food group.

Traditionally, the way to eat from a smorgasbord is to start with the herring, then cold fish dishes, after that some cold meats and salads, then hot food, and finally, cheeses and desserts with coffee.

Glassblower's Herring
Herring Salad
Salted Salmon *(Gravlax)*
Cold Poached Salmon with Mustard-dill Sauce
Boiled Potatoes
Ham Salad
Beet Salad
Cooked Vegetable Salad
Cucumber Salad
Mushroom Salad
Cold Roast Beef
Sliced Smoked Ham
Liver Paté
Jellied Veal Loaf
Jansson's Temptation
Meatballs
Cheeses: Finland Swiss, Blue Cheese, Tilsit-type Cheese, Homemade Milk Cheese
Desserts: May Day Crullers with *Sima*, Cream Pound Cake, Victoria Pudding
Bread: Sour Rye Bread, White Loaf, Mixed Grain Bread, Finn Crisp Crackers
Sima, Beer, Juices, Coffee, Tea, Milk

MIDSUMMER
Juhannus

The nightless night of Finland. Even in southern Finland the sun stays up until about eleven o'clock at night and rises only a couple of hours later. And in between there is a luminous twilight, the earth stands still, the sky is light and the birds don't quite know whether to go to sleep or not. Midsummer in Finland is special.

On Midsummer Eve everyone who has a summer cottage has left the city, families get together, young people go to dances on open air dance floors. The saunas are heated up, and after the bath people sit outside cooling off, enjoying the twilight. Houses are decorated with wildflowers and birch leaves, and at midnight, bonfires are lit on lakesides. Finnish flags are ceremoniously hoisted at 6:00 P.M.; this is the only time of the year that they are allowed to fly through the night and throughout the next day. Many young people celebrate their weddings on Midsummer, allowing families and friends to gather and spend the Midsummer together.

Food in Midsummer festivities tends to be very relaxed, with emphasis on the fresh vegetables that are just starting to arrive at the market, tiny new potatoes and smoked or cold fish. Here is a sample menu:

Summer Vegetable Soup
Cold Poached Salmon with Mustard-dill Sauce or Jellied Veal Loaf
Boiled New Potatoes
Cucumber Salad
Beet Salad
Fresh Egg Cheese
Sour Rye Bread with Butter
Oven Pancake with Strawberry Sauce
Coffee or Tea with *Pulla* and Cookies

CHRISTMAS
Joulu

In November Finland is cold, dark and cloudy. The sun seldom shines and the almost constant cloudy weather makes the darkness of the season even more pronounced. At the beginning of December the sun rises in southern Finland around nine o'clock in the morning and sets at three in the afternoon; in northern Finland sun rises briefly above the horizon, and in the northernmost parts of Finland it does not rise at all, and the land is in constant darkness.

Into this gloomy season Christmas brings light and joy. The darkness disappears into a blaze of lights and candles, the hustle and bustle of preparations has everybody busy, and parties bring people together.

Christmas in Finland starts at the Advent, which is called *pikkujoulu*, or Little Christmas. People light up the first Christmas candles, and from then on every group and company has their own Little Christmas party with food and drink, music and dancing. Streets and businesses are decorated, presents are bought and sometimes handmade, and foods are prepared. Every household tries to make at least a couple of kinds of homemade cookies; breads are baked and some casseroles are prepared early and frozen. Food has to be plentiful, nothing is scrimped on, Christmas is a joyous occasion when tables have to be filled and nothing should be missed. So what, if after the Christmas is over, the belts have to be tightened during what Finns call the lean weeks, or *härkäviikot.*

On the 13th of December Finns of Swedish origin celebrate St. Lucia's day. In families the eldest daughter dons a wreath decorated with candles on her head and a white nightgown, and together with the other children in the family wake up their parents by singing Christmas carols and serving coffee and cakes. Many businesses select their own Lucia and have her preside over coffee parties.

A few days before Christmas, Finns go on a cleaning spree; the house is scrubbed and dusted from top to bottom. It is an old custom that many people still try to adhere to, even with today's busy schedules. In old times clean straw was spread on the floor to remind one of the manger, but nowadays straw is used only for decoration, and in a beautiful delicate mobile hung from the ceiling called *himmeli.* And then of course there is the Christmas tree, most often a fresh spruce, decorated with candles, straw ornaments and sometimes, following an old custom, flags of all nations. And candles; candles are everywhere.

Christmas Eve in Finland is celebrated as the most important part of Christmas. Christmas Eve is the time the main Christmas meal is served, when presents are given and when families gather in front of a decorated Christmas tree, to sing and listen to Christmas carols and light candles to celebrate the holy night.

On Christmas Eve at noon an official Christmas Peace declaration is announced in many cities and towns, the most famous being the one in the Finnish city of Turku, which is broadcast and televised. The message of the declaration is to remind people that this is a holy season when peace should not be disturbed. In the afternoon of the Christmas Eve, Finns who have lost their loved ones gather in cemeteries to light a candle on the grave, and as a result all the cemeteries twinkle full of lights in the early darkness.

The sauna is always heated for Christmas Eve, and after a long and leisurely bath, the Christmas meal is served. After the meal and the caroling and the presents, coffee and glogg are served with cookies and candies. In the old days foods were left on the table for the whole night, so that anybody still hungry after all the feasting could snack through the night. And, of course, the main reason was to provide for the elves. Birds are also not forgotten at Christmas; in the countryside whole sheaves of grain are left for the birds, in cities bird feeders are filled for Christmas.

Church service for Christmas is usually at seven o'clock in the morning, and it is an early wake-up for Christmas morning and a most magical ride to church, since many houses have a candle lit on the windowsill for the benefit of the churchgoers.

Christmas Day is mostly spent resting, and a cold buffet with Christmas foods is served, but the next day, Boxing Day, or St. Stephen's day (*Tapaninpäivä*), which is also a holiday in Finland, is the day when people go visiting each other. An old custom was to go sleigh-riding on St. Stephen's day (*Tapaninajelu*).

Christmas season is officially over on January sixth, the Epiphany, or *Loppiainen*, when the last of the Christmas cookies are eaten and the Christmas tree decorations are taken down. In some parts of the country the season used to extend all the way to January 13th, St. Canute's Day (*Nuutinpäivä*), when children went from house to house dressed up in old clothing asking for treats. After that, Christmas was definitely over, and the cold weeks of winter remained.

Some traditional Finnish foods for the feast follow. The most important meal is on Christmas Eve, and the table is filled with foods. However, present day Finns try to spread out the traditional foods over the three days of Christmas, so that all the specialities can be savored.

Herring Salad
Beet Salad
Salted Salmon (*Gravlax*)
Liver Paté
Jellied Veal Loaf with Pickled Beets and Boiled Potatoes
Lutefisk with White Sauce and Boiled Potatoes
Green Peas
Christmas Ham
Rutabaga Casserole
Mashed Potato Casserole
Carrot and Rice Casserole
Liver and Rice Casserole with Lingonberries
Cabbage and Lingonberry Salad
Christmas Rye Bread
Creamy Rice Porridge with Raisin Soup
Mixed Fruit Pudding or Prune Pudding
Christmas Prune Tarts
Buttermilk Cake
Spice Cookies, Oatmeal Cookies, Cinnamon S-cookies
Rauma Cookies, Aunt Hanna's Cookies
Glogg, Coffee, Tea, Milk, Non-alcoholic Beer

A FINNISH BANQUET
Pidot

An old-fashioned Finnish banquet was held in the countryside for many occasions: weddings, Midsummer festivities or just to see all the members of the extended family together. Banquets were held most often in the summer, when they frequently went on for a couple of days, and sleeping quarters could be provided in unheated farm sheds. Of course, in modern day Finland the banquets have slimmed down considerably, but the old-fashioned big ones are still fondly remembered.

The foods for these occasions have come down many generations and are still served according to the old recipes. In different provinces of Finland foods vary a great deal, and even dishes that are known all over Finland are prepared somewhat differently according to the region. A banquet cook who is an expert in cooking the dishes the way they are traditionally prepared in the region will be invited to take charge of the meals.

In western Finland homemade cheeses are very popular. So is a well made barley porridge. It is cooked for many hours, so that it looks slightly pink and is served with raisin soup or mixed fruit soup. In eastern Finland various pies and pastries baked with meat, vegetables or fish, are prized. In northern Finland baked cheeses and flatbreads are specialties, in central Finland a mashed potato casserole and a special flour mixture called *talkkuna* are served. Here is a typical menu for an old fashioned country gathering:

Often the arriving guests are first treated to a cup of coffee with coffee bread, cakes and cookies to refresh them after a journey. Then a big buffet, *pitopöytä*, is served. It includes various casseroles made with potatoes, rutabagas, macaroni, carrots or liver; beet salad, jellied veal loaf, herring, salted fish, homemade cheeses, meatballs in sauce, sour rye bread, wheat loaves and butter.

Guests are then treated to homemade beef broth with meat pies. For a snack, fruit soups are always available.

The main meal often consists of a pot roast with a cream sauce, potatoes, carrots, and lingonberries. For dessert, barley porridge or rice porridge are often served with raisin soup or blueberry soup.

And of course, it would not be a Finnish feast without coffee and a wealth of coffee breads, cakes and cookies.

And finally, before the guests leave, tea, sandwiches and cakes are offered for the journey home.

At the country banquets, musicians often performed with fiddles and accordions. The drink served throughout, apart from coffee, milk and buttermilk, was homemade non-alcoholic beer called *kalja*, or a somewhat stronger brew, *sahti*.

Since a large part of the Finnish population has moved into the cities during the last few decades, there is not much opportunity to enjoy these customs anymore. However, on a much smaller scale, banquet cooks are still practicing their art, and many young Finns are beginning to see the value of preserving the old traditions.

I.

SOUPS

SUMMER VEGETABLE SOUP
Kesäkeitto

This soup is made with the first crop of summer vegetables, when they are still small and flavorful. You can make the soup with frozen vegetables, but of course some of the flavor will be lost.

4 small carrots, diced
3-4 small new potatoes, diced
1 cup small fresh new peas
1 small head of cauliflower, cut in small florets
2 cups packed fresh spinach leaves, washed, stems removed and coarsely chopped
1 cup fresh pea-pods, stems and strings removed and cut in half
2 teaspoons salt
2 tablespoons butter
2 tablespoons flour
1 cup milk
¼ cup heavy cream
1 egg yolk
¼ teaspoon pepper
2 tablespoons finely chopped fresh dill or parsley

Place the vegetables in a 3-4 quart saucepan with enough boiling water to cover them, add the salt and pepper, and bring back to boil. Lower the heat and simmer until vegetables are tender, about 15 minutes.

In another saucepan melt the butter and stir in the flour. Let cook briefly, then whisk in about 1 cup of the vegetable cooking liquid and the milk. Stir mixture into the vegetables, bring to boil and let simmer for a few minutes. Remove from heat.

In a small bowl mix the egg yolk with the heavy cream. Slowly add about 1 cup of the soup, and pour the mixture back into the soup slowly, stirring continuously. Bring to a near boil, stirring, remove from heat and add the dill or parsley.

SPINACH SOUP
Pinaattikeitto

This soup is often made with young nettles, picked with gloves on and blanched in boiling water to remove the sting.

1 pound fresh spinach or 1 package frozen spinach
2 tablespoons butter
2 tablespoons flour
4 cups vegetable or chicken broth, or water
¼ teaspoon pepper
⅛ teaspoon ground nutmeg
Salt to taste
1 egg yolk
¼ cup heavy cream
1 hard-boiled egg

Wash the spinach well, place in a saucepan, cover tightly and let cook about 5 minutes, until softened. Remove and chop finely.

In another saucepan melt the butter, stir in the flour and let cook briefly. Gradually whisk in the broth or water, let cook for a few minutes, and add the chopped spinach, pepper and nutmeg. Let simmer about 5 minutes and remove from heat. Add salt to taste.

In a small bowl mix the egg yolk with the cream, add about a cupful of the soup and then stir this back into the soup. Heat almost to a boil but do not let boil. Remove from heat. Serve in soup bowls, garnished with sliced or chopped hard-boiled egg.

MUSHROOM SOUP
Sienikeitto

This soup is commonly made with freshly picked wild mushrooms, but common store-bought mushrooms are a perfectly adequate substitute.

1 pound mushrooms, cleaned, stem ends trimmed, and sliced
2 tablespoons butter
3 tablespoons flour
4 cups water
1 teaspoon salt
1 bay leaf
¼ teaspoon dried thyme
¼ teaspoon pepper
¼ cup heavy cream

In a skillet on medium high heat sauté the mushrooms in the butter, stirring, until they are dry and lightly browned. Add the flour and stir briefly to cook the flour. Transfer the mushrooms into a 2-quart saucepan, add the water and the spices, and let simmer for 30 minutes, stirring occasionally. Add the cream and reheat. Add salt to taste.

FISH CHOWDER
Kalakeitto

This soup can be made with almost any fish. The tastiest result comes from using whole cleaned fish, as the bones give more flavor to the broth. Cod steaks are good for this soup, but you can use fish fillets. If you have small fish, clean, gut and remove heads and scales before proceeding.

1½ pounds cleaned fish
3-4 cups water
2 small or 1 medium onion, peeled and sliced
6 whole allspice
1 teaspoon salt
¼ teaspoon white pepper
1 bay leaf

2 carrots, peeled and sliced
6 medium potatoes, peeled and cubed
(Small piece peeled rutabaga)
(A slice of Finnish sourdough rye bread, buttered)
1½-2 cups milk
1 tablespoon flour mixed with ¼ cup cold water
1 tablespoon butter
¼ cup chopped fresh dill

Place the fish in a 3-quart saucepan and add enough water to cover the fish (about 2 cups). Add the onion, allspice, salt, pepper and bay leaf, and bring to simmer. Let the fish simmer gently until it turns opaque and is done, about 15 minutes. Remove the fish to a plate with a slotted spoon. Add the potatoes, carrots, rutabaga and the bread slice into the broth, and more water as needed to cover the vegetables. Cook until the vegetables are tender. Remove the bread slice. Stir the milk and the flour mixture into the soup and heat to simmer. Remove the bones and the skin from the fish and cut it to bite-size pieces. Add the fish pieces in the soup and let them heat through. Dot the soup with butter and sprinkle with chopped dill. Serve in deep soup bowls with fresh bread. Finnish sourdough dark rye with butter is ideal.

BEEF BROTH
Lihaliemi

In winter, what could be more comforting than a hot cup of steaming broth with a slice of meat pie (page 81).

2 pounds beef chuck with bones
1 onion, peeled and quartered
1 carrot, peeled and sliced
1 rib celery, washed and sliced
1 leek, split, washed and sliced
8 cups water

2 teaspoons salt
1 bay leaf
10 whole peppercorns
10 whole allspice

Preheat oven to 400F. Place the meat and the vegetables in a roasting pan and roast, stirring occasionally, until browned, about 1 hour. Do not let the vegetables burn, lower the heat if they seem to be burning. Place the meat and vegetables into a soup pot, add the water, salt and the spices. Bring slowly to a simmer, skimming the surface to remove any froth that forms. Cover and let simmer on very low heat for about 3-4 hours. Strain the soup through a fine-meshed sieve and let cool. Refrigerate the broth and remove the congealed fat on the surface. Heat to serve. Serves 6-8.

BEEF AND POTATO SOUP
Lihakeitto

This soup is the mainstay of Finnish cooking. If you add more potatoes, it is almost like a stew. It is served in all homes, schools and cafeterias. In lean times, when meat was scarce, it was made with beef bones or smoked beef bones.

2 pounds beef chuck with bones
8 cups water
1 whole peeled medium onion
2 teaspoons salt
1 teaspoon whole allspice
1 bay leaf
1 rib celery with leaves
1 leek, split and washed, green top removed
1 small piece of peeled rutabaga or small turnip
2 teaspoons dried marjoram leaves or a couple of fresh sprigs
3 carrots, peeled and sliced

8 medium potatoes, peeled and cut into small chunks
1 tablespoon chopped parsley

Rinse the meat and place in a soup pot with the water. Bring to boil, skimming the surface to remove the froth as it rises to the surface. After most of the froth has disappeared, add the salt, allspice, onion and bay leaf, cover and let simmer for 2 hours. Add the sliced leek, celery, rutabaga and the marjoram and simmer ½ hour. Remove the meat and set it aside to cool, add the carrots and potatoes and simmer another 30-45 minutes, or until the vegetables are tender. Remove the meat from the bones, cut into bite-size pieces and add to the soup. Salt to taste, add the chopped parsley and serve in large bowls, preferably with homemade bread. In Finland it is traditionally served with dark sourdough rye. Serves 6 to 8.

BEEF AND DUMPLING SOUP
Klimppisoppa

This dish is a specialty of western Finland and is often made for special occasions.

1½ pounds beef chuck with bones
6 cups water
1 peeled onion
1 peeled and sliced carrot
1 teaspoon salt
1 teaspoon whole allspice
1 teaspoon dried marjoram leaves
1 bay leaf
Small piece of peeled rutabaga or turnip
1 tablespoon chopped parsley

DUMPLINGS:
3 medium potatoes, preferably Russet
¼ cup broth

½ cup flour
1 large egg
¼-½ teaspoon salt

Place the meat in a pot with cold water, and bring to boil, skimming off the froth as it rises to the surface. Add salt, onion, carrot, allspice, marjoram, bay leaf and rutabaga, cover and simmer for 1½ hours. Add the whole peeled potatoes and simmer until they can be pierced easily with a fork. Remove them from the broth with a slotted spoon to a small bowl and let cool. Mash them with a fork, add ¼ cup of the cooking broth, the egg, flour, and salt. Mix well. When the meat is tender, remove it from the broth and let cool. With a soup spoon dipped in the broth take a rounded tablespoon of the dumpling dough and release it into the broth. If it breaks up, add some more flour to the dough. When the dumpling remains in one piece, drop them all into the broth, dipping the spoon in the broth between dropping each dumpling, and simmer for 5-10 minutes. Remove the bones and fat from the meat, cut it to bite-size pieces and add to the soup. Salt to taste. Add some chopped parsley for color and serve hot in deep soup bowls with bread.

CABBAGE SOUP
Kaalikeitto

2 pounds lamb shoulder chops or lamb shanks; or beef chuck
8 cups water
2 teaspoons salt
1 teaspoon whole allspice berries
½ teaspoon ground pepper
1 bay leaf
1 head of cabbage, core removed and thinly shredded
2 carrots, peeled and sliced
1 onion, peeled and chopped
1 teaspoon dried marjoram leaves

2 tablespoons chopped parsley

Rinse the lamb (or beef) and remove as much visible fat as possible. In a soup pot, bring the meat to boil with the water, salt, pepper, allspice, and bay leaf. Cover and let simmer for 1 hour. Remove the meat from the soup and add the cabbage, carrots, onion and marjoram. Trim the meat from the bones and cut it to bite-size pieces. Add to the soup, and let the soup simmer for about an hour more, or until the vegetables and the meat are tender. Add salt to taste and sprinkle with chopped parsley. Serves 6-8.

DRIED PEA SOUP
Hernekeitto

It has been said that the Finnish army ran on pea soup and hardtack, and it may just be true. Food was scarce in wartime Finland and even the pea soup was often made without meat. This is also a traditional Shrove Tuesday (or Mardi Gras) dish in Finland, followed by Shrove Tuesday buns (page 176) for dessert.

8 cups water
1 pound dried green peas
1-pound piece smoked ham
1 teaspoon dried marjoram leaves
1 onion, peeled and studded with two cloves
1-2 teaspoons salt

Rinse and remove unwanted pieces from the peas, cover them with cold water and let soak overnight. The next day, drain and rinse the peas. Add water and the rest of the ingredients, bring the peas to boil, cover and let simmer until the peas are very soft, about 2 hours, stirring often. Remove the meat from the soup and trim it from the bones, cut it into small pieces and return to the soup. Salt to taste. Serves 6-8.

SAUSAGE SOUP
Makkarakeitto

Sausage soup, made with potatoes as its main ingredient, just as in beef and potato soup, is a very popular Finnish wintertime dish. It is quicker to make than the beef soup, and sausage is a thriftier choice to flavor the soup. There are several different sausages that can be used for this soup, the most popular being a mild pork sausage called siskonmakkara (sister's sausage), but it can be made with a Polish-type sausage, or frankfurters.

6 cups water
2 carrots, peeled and sliced
A small piece of peeled rutabaga
1 rib celery, chopped
1 leek, washed and sliced, green top removed
or 1 onion, peeled and chopped
1 teaspoon salt
¼ teaspoon pepper
6 whole allspice
6 potatoes, peeled and cubed
½-1 pound Polish sausage or frankfurters, sliced
2 tablespoons chopped parsley

Bring the water to boil in a saucepan and add the carrots, rutabaga, celery, onion, salt, pepper, and allspice. Simmer for 15 minutes. Add the potatoes and the sliced leek and let simmer until all the vegetables are tender. Add the sliced sausage and simmer 10 minutes more. Sprinkle with chopped parsley.

BORSCHT
Borssikeitto

This is a Russian dish that migrated to Finland and is still served in restaurants and some homes.

4 medium beets
1 carrot
1 onion
1 pound red or white cabbage (about ½ of a small cabbage)
1 leek
2 tablespoons butter or oil
5 cups beef broth or water
½ teaspoon pepper
1 bay leaf
1 teaspoon marjoram leaves
2 tablespoons wine vinegar
1 teaspoon sugar
(1 teaspoon salt)
(¼ pound Polish sausage or wieners, sliced)
Sour cream

Remove the tops from the beets, pare them and coarsely shred them or cut them into julienne strips. Do the same with the carrot. Peel and chop the onion. With a sharp knife thinly shred the cabbage. Halve and wash the leek well and thinly slice the white part.

In a soup pot lightly brown the vegetables in the oil or butter, add the beef broth or water, pepper, bay leaf and marjoram and simmer the soup until the vegetables are tender, about 45 minutes. Season with vinegar, sugar and salt, if necessary, and add the sausage. Simmer for 5-10 minutes more. Serve with a tablespoon of sour cream to top the soup.

BEER SOUP
Kaljakeitto

Beer soup is traditionally made with a non-alcoholic dark beer called kalja, that is commonly used as a dinner drink in Finland. It is often made without hops, which give beer its bitter flavor. For this dish, use the least bitter dark beer available. This is an old-fashioned dish, that many young Finns have never tasted.

3 cups milk
3 tablespoons flour
1 teaspoon salt
3 cups dark beer
4 tablespoons brown sugar
¾ teaspoon ground ginger

Heat the milk in a nonstick or a thick bottomed saucepan. Mix the flour with ½ cup of cold water and whisk into the milk. Stir until milk thickens slightly. Remove from heat and cover. In another saucepan mix the beer, brown sugar and ginger. Heat to boiling and let simmer for 5 minutes, stirring often. Stir the beer into the milk mixture. Heat the soup to boiling and serve with croutons.

CROUTONS:
4 slices white bread
4 tablespoons butter
Salt and pepper to taste

Toast the bread slices in a toaster and cut into small cubes. In a skillet brown the butter and toss the bread cubes in it until nicely browned. Sprinkle with salt and pepper to taste.

CABBAGE AND MILK SOUP
Maitokaali

1 pound cabbage (about ½ of a small cabbage), shredded with a sharp knife
1 carrot, peeled and sliced
1 tablespoon butter
1½ tablespoons flour
1 cup water
3 cups milk
½ teaspoon ground allspice
1 bay leaf
1 teaspoon salt
1 teaspoon sugar

Melt the butter in a 3-4 quart saucepan, and add the carrot and the cabbage. Toss until coated with butter. Mix in the flour and add the water, milk, allspice and bay leaf. Cover and cook over low heat, stirring often to prevent scorching, until the cabbage is soft, about 45 minutes. Season with salt and sugar.

II.
FISH

SALTED SALMON (*Gravlax*)
Graavi lohi

No smorgasbord in Finland is complete without salt-cured fish, be it salmon or whitefish. Whitefish prepared this way is especially popular in western Finland. The fish is sliced and served with hot boiled potatoes or on a sandwich.

2 salmon fillets with skin (about 2 pounds)
3 tablespoons coarse (kosher) salt, or if not available, substitute non-iodized table salt
3 tablespoons sugar
2 teaspoons crushed white peppercorns (or substitute black peppercorns)
1 large bunch fresh dill

Make sure the fish for this dish is very fresh. Wipe the fish clean with paper towels, do not rinse the fish. Mix the salt, sugar and the pepper together and rub the fish all over with the mixture. The thicker parts of the fish need more salt mixture. Place one fillet on a shallow glass or stainless steel dish skin side down. Rinse the dill and pat dry with paper towels. Spread evenly over the fish. Place the other fillet skin side up over the fish, placing the thinner end over the thick end. Cover with plastic wrap, and put a weight over the fish, such as a plate topped with food cans. Refrigerate for 24 to 48 hours. Turn the fish over a couple of times during this time and baste it with the liquid that accumulates, spooning some liquid to the inside also. Keep the fish covered and weighted.

Remove the fish from the marinade and scrape off the seasonings. Place a fillet on a cutting board skin side down and cut thin slices diagonally off the skin, keeping the knife very flat. Serve with fresh dill and lemon wedges as an appetizer or with boiled potatoes and mustard-dill sauce as a main course.

MUSTARD-DILL SAUCE
Sinappi-tillikastike

2 tablespoons Dijon-type mustard
2 tablespoons hot water
¼ cup vegetable oil
¼ cup heavy cream
2 teaspoons sugar
Salt to taste
¼ cup finely chopped fresh dill

In a small bowl using a wire whisk beat the mustard with the hot water until well mixed. Gradually dribble in the oil, beating until the sauce thickens. Mix in the cream. Season with sugar, salt and chopped dill.

POACHED SALMON
Keitetty lohi

4-6 salmon steaks or 1½-2 pounds salmon fillets
Water to cover
1 small onion, peeled and sliced
2 tablespoons lemon juice
1 bay leaf
3-4 whole white peppercorns
½ teaspoon salt per 1 cup water

In a skillet bring the water to boil with the seasonings and simmer for 5 minutes. Add the salmon and poach the salmon on a gentle simmer for about 10-20 minutes, or until the fish flakes easily. Drain the fish and make a sauce with the cooking liquid. Serve hot with mustard sauce or cold with mustard-dill sauce.

MUSTARD SAUCE
Sinappikastike

2 tablespoons butter
2 tablespoons flour
2 cups water and fish cooking liquid
1 tablespoon Dijon-type mustard
1 tablespoon lemon juice
1 tablespoon heavy cream
Salt to taste
2 tablespoons chopped dill

Melt the butter in the saucepan, stir in the flour and let cook briefly, stirring. Whisk in the water and the fish cooking liquid, and cook until thickens. Season with the mustard, lemon juice, heavy cream, chopped dill, and salt, if needed. Serve with fish pudding or poached salmon.

SALMON PIE
Lohipiirakka

PASTRY:
12 tablespoons butter or margarine (1½ sticks)
2 cups flour
½ pound cream cheese or Neufchâtel cheese (light cream cheese)

Blend the butter and flour together until the mixture resembles coarse meal. Work in the cream cheese until the dough holds together in a ball. Wrap and chill for 30 minutes.

FILLING:
1 tablespoon butter or oil
1 small onion, peeled and chopped
¾ cup uncooked rice
1½ cup chicken broth or water

2 cups canned or fresh salmon
2 hard-boiled eggs, peeled and coarsely chopped
½ cup chopped fresh dill
Salt and pepper to taste
2 tablespoons milk or cream
1 tablespoon lemon juice

GLAZE:
1 egg yolk
2 tablespoons milk

Melt the butter in a saucepan and add the chopped onion. Cook until the onion is soft. Add the rice and stir until rice is coated with butter. Add the chicken broth or water, bring to boil, cover, and let cook over low heat for 18 minutes.

While the rice is cooking, remove the skin and bones from the salmon, coarsely flake it, and add the chopped eggs and half of the chopped dill. Sprinkle with salt to taste.

After the rice is cooked, fluff it with a fork and stir in the rest of the chopped dill. If the mixture seems dry, add a couple of tablespoons of milk or cream, and sprinkle with pepper and salt, if needed.

Preheat oven to 375°F. Divide the pastry dough in roughly two equal pieces, making one part slightly bigger than the other. Roll the smaller piece on top of a parchment paper the size of a cookie sheet (dampen the surface underneath with water to prevent slipping) to a size approximately 6x10 inches. Transfer the paper with the dough on it onto a cookie sheet. Spoon the rice mixture evenly over the dough, leaving about one inch of dough visible all around. Spoon the salmon mixture evenly over the rice and sprinkle lemon juice over the salmon. Roll the other half of dough into a slightly larger sheet than the first one and transfer it with the aid of a rolling pin on top of the salmon. Press the edges firmly together with the aid of a fork. You may decorate the surface by lightly drawing the tines of the fork over the surface, crisscrossing both ways. Beat the egg yolk with the milk and brush the loaf before baking. Bake for about 45 minutes, or until golden brown. Serve hot in slices, with melted butter or sour cream.

BOILED COD WITH EGG SAUCE
Keitetty turska munakastikkeella

Pike is the fish most often used for this dish in Finland, but cod is a good substitute.

2 pounds cod fillets
1 cup milk
1 small onion, sliced
1 bay leaf
½ teaspoon salt
⅛ teaspoon white pepper

FOR THE SAUCE:
3 tablespoons butter
3 tablespoons flour
2½ cups fish cooking liquid
3 tablespoons heavy cream
2 hard-boiled eggs, chopped
Chopped parsley or dill

Cut the fillets into serving pieces. Place them in a skillet large enough to hold them in one layer. Add the milk and enough water to just cover, the sliced onion, the bay leaf and sprinkle with salt and pepper. Bring to a simmer but do not let come to a full boil. Reduce heat and gently poach the fish until it turns opaque and flakes easily. Remove the pieces with a slotted spoon to a warm serving dish and keep warm while you are making the sauce.

Strain the cooking liquid. Melt the butter in a saucepan, add the flour and let cook briefly. Gradually add fish cooking liquid, stirring with a wire whisk, until the sauce is smooth and thickened. Add the cream, and if the sauce seems too thick, a little more cooking liquid. Add the finely chopped eggs and salt, if needed. Serve the sauce with the fish. Garnish the dish with chopped parsley or chopped dill.

FISH PUDDING
Kalamureke

1 pound cod fillets
2 tablespoons butter, softened
2 large eggs
1 tablespoon flour
1 tablespoon potato starch or cornstarch
1 teaspoon salt
¼ teaspoon ground white pepper
1 tablespoon lemon juice
½-¾ cup heavy cream

Preheat oven to 350°F. Make sure all the bones have been removed from the fish. In a food processor grind the fish with the other ingredients adding enough cream to make a smooth mixture. Spoon the mixture into a buttered 1-quart mold and set the mold into a larger pan with hot water. Bake about 1 hour, or until knife plunged in the middle comes out clean. Let the pudding rest for 5 minutes before unmolding. If there is liquid around the pudding in the mold, drain it off and use it in the sauce. Place a serving dish over the mold and invert the mold over the serving dish. Decorate with lemon wedges and dill and serve with mustard sauce (page 52) or shrimp sauce (page 62).

BAKED COD
Kuorrutettu turska

This dish can be successfully made with almost any fish, except the very oily ones. Use a slice of a large fish or fish fillets, or cleaned whole fish. With whole fish you have to adjust the cooking time accordingly.

2 pounds fish slices or whole fish or 1½ pounds fish fillets
Salt and white pepper
2 tablespoons melted butter
3 tablespoons dry bread crumbs
½ cup grated Finland Swiss cheese
½ cup heavy cream or milk
2 tablespoons chopped parsley or dill

Preheat oven to 350°F. Place the fish slices on a buttered baking dish. Brush with melted butter and pour the cream or milk over the fish. Sprinkle with salt, pepper, bread crumbs and the cheese. Bake for 30 minutes, or until the cheese is melted and browned and the fish flakes easily. If necessary to brown the topping, run quickly under a broiler. Sprinkle with chopped parsley or dill.

BAKED FILLED PIKE
Täytetty uunihauki

A 3-3½ pound pike or sea bass, cleaned and scaled
1 package (10 ounces) frozen spinach, or 1 pound fresh spinach, well rinsed
Salt and pepper
4 tablespoons butter
2 hard-boiled eggs, peeled and chopped
Juice of half a lemon
4 tablespoons dry bread crumbs
2 tablespoons chopped fresh dill

Preheat oven to 375°F and prepare the filling: Quickly cook the spinach in water, drain and squeeze as much moisture out as possible. Add 1 tablespoon butter to the hot spinach and sprinkle with salt and pepper. Mix in the chopped eggs and fill the fish with the mixture. For bigger fish you may add some cooked rice to this mixture. Close the fish with toothpicks.

Melt the rest of the butter in a baking pan and turn the fish in it until coated on both sides with the butter. Sprinkle with salt and pepper and sprinkle on the lemon juice and the bread crumbs. Bake for about 45 minutes, or until the fish loosens easily from the bone. Baste frequently with pan juices during cooking and add some water in the pan during cooking, if the juices seem to evaporate. When cooked, place on a serving dish, sprinkle with fresh dill and serve with lemon wedges.

SAUTÉED FISH WITH CREAM SAUCE
Paistettu kala kermakastikkeessa

In Finland this dish is made with pike or perch, but if these are not available, you can make it with ocean perch or halibut.

1½-2 pounds whole cleaned fish, fish steaks or fish fillets
1 cup rye flour or all-purpose flour
2-3 tablespoons butter
Dill sprigs
½-¾ cup half-and-half or cream
Salt and pepper to taste

Rinse the fish and pat dry. Put the flour on a plate and roll the fish to coat. In a skillet quickly sauté the fish in butter until golden brown on both sides. Sprinkle with salt and pepper, and place dill sprigs on top of the fish. Add the half-and-half to the skillet, cover, and let slowly simmer for a few minutes, or until the fish flakes easily. Add some more half-and-half or cream, if needed, to make a few spoonfuls of sauce for every portion. Add salt to taste. Serve with boiled potatoes and dark rye bread.

BAKED HALIBUT
Uunikala

1 slice (about 1-1½ pounds) halibut or a 1-1½-pound cod fillet with bones removed
1 tablespoon melted butter
1 large ripe tomato, thinly sliced
1 small onion, peeled and thinly sliced
⅓ cup heavy cream
Salt and pepper

Preheat oven to 350°F. Carefully cut the skin and bones off the halibut, or leave it whole, if you prefer. Place the fish slice on a buttered baking dish and brush with the melted butter. Sprinkle with salt and freshly ground pepper and layer the tomato slices and the onion slices on the fish. Bake for 20 minutes. Pour the heavy cream over the fish and bake 10 minutes more. Serve with boiled potatoes.

SAUTÉED FLOUNDER
Paistettu kampela

4 fillets of flounder or gray sole
1 cup milk
Flour for dredging
2 tablespoons vegetable oil
4 tablespoons butter
1 lemon
Sprigs of fresh dill

On a plate, soak the flounder fillets in the milk for a few minutes. Drain and dredge in the flour on another plate. Melt 2 tablespoons of the butter and the oil in a skillet and cook the fish on medium heat on both sides until golden brown. Place the fish on a warm platter, melt the rest of the butter in the pan until sizzling, and pour over the fish. Decorate with lemon wedges and sprigs of dill. Serve with boiled potatoes.

FISH CASSEROLE
Kalalaatikko

This dish is customarily made with salted Baltic herring or salted salmon, but it can also be made with rainbow trout. Have the fish filleted, place it on a plate and sprinkle liberally with salt. Cover it with plastic wrap and refrigerate a few hours before proceeding with the recipe. Some people also like to layer a few slices of salt pork with the fish.

6 cups sliced raw potatoes
1 pound fish fillets, bones removed and cut into 1-inch pieces
1 medium onion, peeled and chopped
1-2 teaspoons salt
½ teaspoon ground white pepper or black pepper
½ teaspoon ground allspice
1 tablespoon flour
3 cups milk
2 eggs
¼ cup dry bread crumbs
2 tablespoons butter

Preheat oven to 350°F. In a buttered heatproof shallow casserole layer the potatoes with the fish pieces and the chopped onion. Sprinkle each layer with pepper, allspice, flour and salt, keeping in mind that fish already has some salt in it. Top with a layer of potatoes. Beat the eggs with the milk and pour over the potatoes. Sprinkle with bread crumbs and distribute pieces of butter over on top. Bake in 350°F oven for 1½ hours, or until the top is nicely browned and potatoes are tender.

JANSSON'S TEMPTATION
Janssonin kiusaus

There is a story about the name of this dish. It seems there was a religious zealot named Jansson, who preached abstinence and self-control over worldly pleasures. Unfortunately, he himself had a temptation he was unable to resist....

6 medium baking potatoes
2 medium onions, peeled and thinly sliced
3½-ounce can Swedish anchovy fillets
2 tablespoons butter
3 tablespoons dry bread crumbs
1 cup heavy cream

Preheat oven to 400°F. Sauté the onions in a skillet in 2 tablespoons of butter until soft and translucent. Peel and thinly slice the potatoes, stack the slices and cut the potatoes into matchsticks. Put them into a bowl of cold water and rinse them well. Drain, and pat them dry with paper towels. Layer the matchstick potatoes with the onions and anchovy fillets in a buttered shallow casserole, making the last layer potatoes. Sprinkle with the bread crumbs. Bake for 20 minutes. Pour the cream over the potatoes and cook for another 20-25 minutes. If the crumbs seem to be burning, lower the heat a little.

Note: If you are unable to find the Swedish anchovies, you can use the regular canned anchovies. The taste is not exactly the same, but the dish is still delicious.

CUSTARD ROLL WITH SMOKED FISH FILLING
Kalarulla

This lunch dish may also be made with different fillings. For instance, a thick mushroom sauce makes a very nice filling.

2 cups milk
6 tablespoons flour, preferably granulated
6 large eggs
½ teaspoon salt
½ cup grated Finland Swiss cheese

Preheat oven to 400°F. In a large bowl beat the milk gradually into the flour, beat in the eggs and season with salt. Line a 10"x15" jelly roll pan with parchment paper all the way up to the sides, butter it, and pour the batter in. Bake for about 20 minutes, or until puffed and lightly browned. Invert the pan onto another sheet of parchment paper and peel the top paper off. Let cool for 5-10 minutes.

Spread the filling over the custard, roll it up, sprinkle with cheese and bake in 400°F oven for 20 minutes, or until heated through and the cheese has melted. Serve in thick slices, with a salad.

FILLING:
1 pound smoked cooked fish, picked clean of skin and bones
4 tablespoons chopped fresh dill
4 tablespoons heavy cream
Salt and pepper to taste

Flake the fish with a fork and mix with the dill and the cream. Add salt and pepper, if needed. Spread on the custard roll.

CRAYFISH BOILED WITH DILL
Keitetyt ravut

Finns love their crayfish and when the season starts in July, crayfish parties are arranged at home and in restaurants. Finnish crayfish are small, similar to the fresh-water crayfish available in the southern and midwestern United States. Eating crayfish is always an occasion, and they are consumed in great quantities accompanied with buttered toast, icy vodka and beer. Since they are eaten with fingers, plenty of paper napkins to tie under the chin are necessary, and often just a coffee and dessert follow the feast. About 10 crayfish per diner are customary.

40 live fresh-water crayfish
5 quarts water
⅓ cup coarse (kosher) salt, or if not available, regular non-iodized salt
Dill blossoms and seed pods, or dill crowns, as they are called in Finland, or if they are not available, substitute 4 tablespoons dill seed tied in a cheesecloth and 3 bunches of fresh dill.

In an 8-quart kettle bring the water to boil with the salt, dill seeds and 2 tied bunches of fresh dill, saving a few sprigs for decoration. Simmer for 10 minutes. Check that the crayfish are live and discard any dead ones. Rinse them well under running water. Bring the water in the kettle to a full rolling boil and drop the crayfish, a few at a time, into the boiling water. When all the crayfish are in the kettle, and the water again boils, cover it tightly and let boil for 7-8 minutes.

Spread the last bunch of fresh dill into a large 4-5 quart bowl and remove the crayfish from the kettle with a slotted spoon into the bowl. Strain the cooking liquid over on top of the crayfish, and let them cool in the liquid. Cover the bowl and refrigerate for 10-12 hours, or up to 24 hours. Remove the crayfish from the broth and pile them high on a serving dish. Decorate with fresh dill.

SHRIMP WITH DILL SAUCE
Katkarapumuhennos

In Scandinavia shrimp means the tiny crustaceans available in the North Sea; luckily they are available canned. This sauce is often served with Fish Pudding (page 55), or as an appetizer with toast triangles, or as a filling for patty shells.

2 tablespoons butter
2 tablespoons flour
1½ cups milk or half and half
Salt and white pepper to taste
2 teaspoons Dijon-style mustard
1 tablespoon lemon juice
½ cup chopped fresh dill
½ pound cooked, peeled small shrimp, or 2 cans (4½-ounce size) tiny shrimp, rinsed and drained.

In a saucepan melt the butter, stir in the flour and let cook briefly. Stir in the milk and let the sauce cook a few minutes. If you are going to use it as a sauce for the fish pudding, add a few tablespoons milk to thin out the sauce. Stir in the seasonings and salt and pepper to taste, and add the rinsed shrimp. If you use the sauce for an appetizer, save a few shrimp and a few dill sprigs for decoration.

FISH PIE
Kalakukko

Kalakukko is a famous dish of the Savo province in eastern Finland. The pie is a big pile of fish and pork wrapped in rye dough and baked in the oven for hours. In Finland it is made with the small sweetwater fish called muikku, or sometimes with other kinds of small fish that are too time-consuming to bone. Since the pie cooks for several hours in the oven, the bones soften and become part of the dish.

2 cups water
1½ teaspoons salt
2 cups flour
4 cups rye flour

4 tablespoons melted butter or margarine

FILLING:

2 pounds smelts, small perch, or whitefish fillets, cleaned, heads and scales removed, and dried in paper towels
6 ounces sliced fresh pork side, or salt pork, or substitute bacon which has been simmered in water for 10 minutes to remove an excessively smoky taste, rinsed and dried
1-2 teaspoons salt
2-3 tablespoons rye flour

Preheat oven to 400°F. Mix the flours with the salt, water and melted butter, and knead until you get a fairly stiff dough. On a floured board shape the dough into a round ball, sprinkle it with flour, flatten it with hands and roll out with a rolling pin into a large oval about ½ inch thick. Save a small piece of dough for mending the pie.

Sprinkle some rye flour in the center of the dough. Layer the fish with the pork, sprinkling each layer with a little salt and rye flour. Do not use too much salt, if you are using salt pork or bacon. Make the top layer pork.

Fold the sides over the fish and with hands dipped in water seal the seams of the dough. Sprinkle the pie with rye flour and smooth it dry. Place it on a baking sheet covered with parchment paper and bake for about 45 minutes, or until slightly browned. Remove the pie from oven and mend the pie with pieces of the dough, if the juices run out of the pie. Wrap the pie in parchment paper, then in aluminum foil, and return to oven. Lower the heat to 275°F and bake the pie for 4-5 hours more.

To serve, cut the top crust off the pie, scoop out some of the filling and serve pieces of the crust with the fish, along with some melted butter and lemon wedges, if desired.

LUTEFISK
Lipeäkala

This dish is part of the traditional Christmas menu. Its origins go back a few centuries to Catholic Sweden, to which Finland belonged at the time. It is made from sun dried codfish soaked in lye solution, and well rinsed. Admittedly, that does not sound as appetizing as it is; the fish actually has a mild taste and a slightly crunchy texture that is loved by many. There are some stores catering to Scandinavian customers, which stock lutefisk during the Christmas season.

3 pounds lutefisk
Water to cover
1 teaspoon salt
A few peppercorns

Rinse the lutefisk well and place in a stainless steel or enameled saucepan. Cover with water, add salt and peppercorns. Heat, but do not let come to full boil. Cover and slowly poach the fish for 15 minutes, or until it flakes easily and is translucent. Drain carefully and put on a serving platter. Serve napped with white sauce and sprinkled with ground allspice or black pepper.

WHITE SAUCE
Valkokastike

2 tablespoons butter
3 tablespoons flour
2½ cups milk
¾ teaspoon salt
¼ teaspoon ground white pepper

Melt the butter in a saucepan, add the flour and cook briefly. Remove the pan from heat, add the milk all at once while beating with a wire whip, return to heat, bring to boil and simmer for 5 minutes, stirring. Add salt and white pepper to taste. Serve with lutefisk.

III.

MEATS AND POULTRY

POT ROAST
Patapaisti

Bottom round is a very good piece of meat for this dish, but you can make it with any lean, compact piece of beef, e.g. sirloin tip or rump roast. Long cooking time makes the meat very soft, and it is easier to slice if you let it stand for a while before serving.

3-4 pound piece of bottom round roast
2 tablespoons butter
1 medium onion
1 carrot
4 cups beef broth or water
1 large bay leaf
1 teaspoon whole allspice
¼ cup flour, preferably granulated
2 tablespoons heavy cream
Salt to taste

Preheat oven to 350°F. Trim all fat from the meat and tie it up in a couple of places with cotton twine. This makes it easier to handle. Melt the butter in a 4-5 quart casserole in which the meat fits easily, and brown the meat on all sides. Remove it from the casserole, add the onion and carrot and cook until the onion softens and is lightly browned. Put the meat back in the casserole, add the water or broth and bring to boil. Add the bay leaf and allspice, and 1 teaspoon salt if you have not used broth, cover and cook in oven for 3-4 hours, turning the meat once after two hours.

When meat is very soft when tested with a fork, remove the casserole from the oven, take the meat out of the casserole and keep warm.

To make sauce: Strain the broth through a sieve into a saucepan and bring it to boil. You should have about 3 cups of the broth, add more water, if necessary. Mix the flour with ½ cup of cold water until there are no lumps, and whisk the flour mixture gradually into the boiling broth. Let simmer over low heat for

10-15 minutes. Stir in the heavy cream and add salt if needed. Slice the meat thinly and serve with the sauce. Mashed potatoes are a good accompaniment for this dish (page 98). Serves 6-8.

BEEF RAGOUT
Palapaisti

2 pounds bottom round or top round of beef, cut into 1-inch cubes
1 tablespoon vegetable oil
1 tablespoon butter
2 medium onions, peeled and chopped
2 carrots, peeled and sliced
1 rib celery, peeled and sliced
2 cups water
1 teaspoon salt
½ teaspoon ground allspice
½ teaspoon pepper
2 bay leaves
2-3 tablespoons heavy cream
3 tablespoons flour, preferably granulated
⅓ cup cold water

In a skillet, brown the beef cubes on all sides, a few at a time, in the mixture of butter and oil. Transfer into a casserole. Lightly brown the onions and the vegetables in the same skillet and add into the casserole. Rinse the skillet with the water and pour over the meat in the casserole. Add the salt and the spices. Cover and let cook over low heat or in a 325°F oven for 2 hours, or until the meat is tender. Mix the flour with the cold water and stir into the casserole along with the cream. Let simmer for 5 minutes more. Add salt to taste. Serve with boiled potatoes. Browned rutabagas (page 101) and pickled pumpkin (page 120) are frequently served with this dish.

BEEF STROGANOFF
Stroganoff

Beef Stroganoff is normally made with beef fillet, which is quickly sautéed. In Finland, however, it is most often made with lesser cuts of meat, which are braised and flavored with Stroganoff flavorings.

1½ pounds top round of beef, cut into ½-inch cubes
2 tablespoons vegetable oil or butter
1 medium onion, peeled and chopped
½ teaspoon pepper
1 teaspoon salt
1 tablespoon tomato paste
1 bay leaf
1½ cups water
¼ cup cream
2 tablespoons flour, preferably granulated
½ cup finely chopped cucumber pickles or sour gherkins (cornichons) and 1-2 tablespoons of the brine from the jar
½ cup sour cream

In a skillet over high heat brown the beef cubes on all sides in half the oil or butter, a few at a time, and transfer them to a casserole. Lower the heat and in the same skillet cook the onion in the rest of the butter or oil, until soft and lightly browned. Add onion to the casserole along with the salt, pepper, tomato paste, and bay leaf. Rinse the skillet with the water and pour it on top of the meat in the casserole. Cover and simmer the meat for about 1 hour, or until it is tender. Mix the flour with the cream, stir into the casserole, and cook until the sauce thickens, then stir in the chopped pickles, brine, and sour cream. Serve with boiled potatoes or rice.

SAILOR'S STEAK CASSEROLE
Merimiespihvi

The name obviously refers to the lack of steaks on board old-fashioned ships. This is your basic meat and potatoes casserole with the addition of beer, and very tasty it is.

1 pound lean beef round or brisket
2 tablespoons butter or vegetable oil
3 medium onions, peeled and thinly sliced
8 medium potatoes
2 teaspoons salt
¼ teaspoon pepper
½ teaspoon ground allspice
1 cup beer
1 cup beef broth
1 bay leaf
1 tablespoon chopped parsley

Preheat oven to 350°F. Cut the meat into thin slices and in a hot skillet brown them quickly on both sides in half the butter or oil. If you use a nonstick skillet, no butter is necessary. After you have browned the meat slices, remove them to a plate, lower the heat, and brown the onions slowly in the rest of the butter until they are soft and golden. Peel and slice the potatoes. In a casserole layer the potatoes with the browned meat and onions, sprinkling each meat layer with a little salt, pepper and allspice. Make the last layer one of potatoes. Rinse the skillet with the beer and the broth and pour in the casserole. Add the bay leaf. Cover tightly and place the casserole in oven for 1-1½ hours, or until the meat is tender. Sprinkle with parsley and serve directly from the casserole, traditionally with pickled beets (page 119).

KARELIAN HOT POT
Karjalanpaisti

This is an easy dish to make because you can start it at lunchtime and have it ready for dinner. In the days of wood-burning ovens in Karelia, this dish was made after bread had been baked and the leftover oven heat was not to be wasted. The proportions of the meats are somewhat flexible; you can take whatever meats are available, but it is best with at least two different kinds of meat.

1 pound beef chuck, cut in 1-inch cubes
1 pound lamb shoulder, cut in 1-inch cubes
1 pound pork shoulder, cut in 1-inch cubes
1 onion, peeled and quartered
1 bay leaf
1 teaspoon whole allspice
2-3 teaspoons salt
½ cup water

Preheat oven to 275°F. Use a heavy casserole or pot with a tight-fitting lid. Place the meat in the pot with the onion, bay leaf, allspice and water. Sprinkle with salt. Use a smaller amount first, and add to taste later on. Cover tightly, place the casserole in oven and let cook for 5 hours, stirring once. You should not need any more water, but if the meat seems to be drying out, add some more. The meat should basically cook in its own juices. Serve with boiled potatoes, fresh rye bread and a salad, if desired.

ROAST BEEF
Paahtopaisti

A rib roast with 2 ribs
(1 clove garlic, peeled and cut in half)
Salt and freshly ground pepper

Have the butcher remove the bones and the fat covering the roast and tie it into a roll, or do it yourself. Heat the oven to 350°F. Rub the roast all over with the garlic clove, if desired, and sprinkle the roast with salt and plenty of pepper. Place it in the bottom of a small roasting pan. Do not use a rack. Insert a meat thermometer with the tip in the thickest part of the meat. Place it in the oven. In about 30 minutes turn the roast over. Check when the juices from the roast start to brown and add ½ cup of water. Cook to an internal temperature of 130°F, about 1 hour to 1 hour 15 minutes, depending on the size of the roast and the oven. Add more water in the roasting pan as needed, if it seems to be evaporating.

When the roast is cooked, remove from oven and cover to keep it warm. Let sit for 15 minutes. Remove the roast to a serving platter, take off the strings, and place the roasting pan over heat. Scrape the browned bits into the broth in the pan; if necessary add some more water to make about ¾ cup. Skim the fat from the broth, add salt if needed, and strain it into a sauceboat. Serve the roast in thin slices with a spoonful of the broth.

BOILED BEEF WITH HORSERADISH SAUCE
Piparjuuriliha

2 pounds stewing beef, cubed
4 cups water
2 teaspoons salt
1 onion, peeled and quartered
1 teaspoon whole allspice
1 bay leaf

In a saucepan bring the meat to boil in the water, skimming off the froth that rises to the surface. Add the salt, onion, allspice and bay leaf, cover, and let simmer until the meat is tender, about 1½-2 hours. Drain and reserve the broth. Cover the meat to keep it warm while the sauce is prepared.

SAUCE:

2 tablespoons butter
3 tablespoons flour
2½ cups meat broth
1 tablespoon sugar
2 tablespoons prepared horseradish, or 1 tablespoon white vinegar and grated fresh horseradish to taste

Melt the butter in a saucepan. Add the flour and let it cook briefly, stirring continuously. Whisk in the meat broth and the seasonings and let simmer for 5-10 minutes. Add more seasonings if needed, pour over the reserved meat and serve with boiled potatoes.

CABBAGE ROLLS
Kaalikääryleet

3-pound head of cabbage
Water, salt

FILLING:

¾ cup rice
1½ cups water
1 onion, chopped
1 tablespoon vegetable oil or butter
1 pound ground beef
1 large egg
2 cups chopped inner leaves from the cabbage
½ cup cream or half-and-half
1 cup cabbage cooking water
2 teaspoons salt
½ teaspoon pepper
1 teaspoon dried marjoram leaves
2 cups beef broth or cabbage cooking water
1 tablespoon heavy cream

ON TOP:
2 tablespoons melted butter
2 tablespoons dark corn syrup or pancake syrup

Carefully cut as much of the core as you can out of the cabbage with a small knife. This allows water to enter the cabbage and cooks it faster. Take a pot big enough to fit the cabbage comfortably, pour boiling water to cover, add salt to taste, bring to boil and let cook slowly 10-15 minutes, or until the cabbage leaves soften. Take the cabbage out onto a dish and let cool. Save the cooking water.

In a small saucepan, bring the water and rice to boil, lower the heat, stir once, cover and simmer for 18 minutes. Let cool.

Preheat oven to 350°F. Cook the chopped onion in the oil or butter until soft and lightly browned. In a mixing bowl combine the rice, onion, meat and egg. Loosen the leaves carefully from the cabbage one at a time. You should have about 15 leaves. Finely chop the broken ones and the small inner ones, and add to the meat and rice. Add the cream or half-and-half and enough of the cooking water to make a fairly loose mixture. Season with salt, pepper and marjoram.

Thin out the stems of the cabbage leaves, spread the leaves out and fill each one with a full tablespoonful of the filling. Fold the sides in and roll up the leaves around the filling. Arrange the cabbage rolls into an oiled roasting pan, baste with the butter, drizzle the syrup over the rolls and bake for1½-2 hours.

Midway through the baking turn the rolls over and add the broth or water to the pan. Keep adding some cooking water into the pan, if the liquid seems to be evaporating. When cooked and nicely brown, remove the rolls from the pan. Scrape off all the bits at the bottom of the pan and strain the liquid. Add 1-2 tablespoons heavy cream to the juices and more salt, if needed. Heat and pour over the rolls. Serve with lingonberries, if available.

CABBAGE CASSEROLE
Kaalilaatikko

This contains basically the same ingredients as cabbage rolls, but is less time-consuming to prepare.

1 2-to-3-pound head of cabbage
Water, salt
¾ cup rice
1½ cups water
1 onion, peeled and chopped
1 tablespoon butter
1 pound lean ground beef
1 teaspoon salt
½ teaspoon pepper
½ teaspoon ground allspice
1 large egg
1½-2 cups milk
2 tablespoons dark corn syrup or pancake syrup
1 teaspoon dried marjoram leaves

With a sharp knife thinly shred the cabbage and place it into a 4-quart pot with 2 cups of water and 1 teaspoon salt. Cover tightly and steam the cabbage until it is wilted, about 10-15 minutes. Pour out the cooking water but save it.

In a saucepan place the rice with 1½ cups water, bring to boil, stir once, cover and let simmer for 18 minutes. Add the rice to the cabbage.

Heat oven to 325°F. In a skillet cook the onion in butter until lightly browned. Add the ground beef and cook it while breaking it up into small crumbs with a fork or a spatula. When the meat is lightly browned, season it with the salt, pepper and allspice. Stir ½ cup of water into the skillet and scrape off all the browned bits at the bottom of the skillet. Mix the meat with the cabbage.

Beat the egg with the milk and stir it to the cabbage mixture with enough of the cooking liquid and milk to make a fairly loose mixture. Add the syrup and marjoram, and salt, if needed.

Turn the mixture into a buttered casserole and cook in oven for 1 hour. Cover the casserole to prevent too much browning and cook 1 hour more. Serve with lingonberries or with cranberry sauce.

MEATBALLS
Lihapyörykät

Every family has its own recipe for the meatballs. This is a basic recipe, to which many people add chopped dill, chives, parsley, cheese, cream—the combinations are endless. Since the dough is very soft, it is almost impossible to make the meatballs perfectly round. If you want to serve them in a smorgasbord, make them a little smaller, without the sauce.

2 pounds lean ground beef
4 slices white bread, crumbled
1 cup milk or club soda
1 large onion or 2 smaller ones, peeled and chopped
4 tablespoons butter
2 teaspoons salt
1 teaspoon ground allspice
2 large eggs
2 tablespoons flour
2 cups beef broth or water
2 tablespoons heavy cream

In a bowl, soak the crumbled bread in the milk. Sauté the chopped onion in 2 tablespoons of the butter until soft and lightly browned. Add to the bowl with the meat, salt, allspice and eggs. Beat well with a wooden spoon or with an electric mixer. Chill for 15 minutes. With hands dipped in cold water form small balls and brown them in rest of the butter in a skillet, turning them often. If you are serving them without the sauce, cover the skillet and let them cook over low heat an additional 15 minutes, adding perhaps a tablespoon or two of water, to prevent burning.

For the Sauce: Remove the meatballs from the skillet and all but 2 tablespoons of the drippings. Stir in the flour and cook briefly. Add the broth or water, and the cream, and cook until the sauce thickens. Add the meatballs to the sauce, cover and let simmer for 15 minutes. Add salt to taste.

Another way to make the sauce is to pour out the fat in the skillet, stir in the broth and cream and 2 tablespoons of flour mixed with ¼ cup water. Continue stirring, and after the sauce thickens, add salt to taste, and the meatballs, cover and cook for 15 minutes.

Meatballs are traditionally served with lingonberries, boiled potatoes, and often a cucumber salad. Serves 6-8.

MEAT LOAF
Lihamureke

Finnish meat loaf is traditionally formed into a loaf and cooked in an open pan, so that it browns all over. Any kind of brown sauce can be served with it, but creamed mushrooms (page 104) are always a favorite.

2 pounds lean ground beef
4 slices of white bread, crumbled
1 cup milk
1 large onion or 2 small ones, peeled and chopped
2 tablespoon butter or vegetable oil
2 teaspoons salt
1 teaspoon ground allspice
2 large eggs
½ cup grated Swiss cheese

In a bowl, soak the crumbled bread in the milk. Sauté the onion in butter or oil until soft and lightly browned. Add it into the bowl with the meat, salt, allspice and eggs. Beat with a wooden spoon or an electric mixer until fluffy. Chill for 30 minutes.

Preheat oven to 350°F. With hands dipped in cold water lift the dough into a roasting pan, shape it into a high loaf (it flattens out as it cooks), sprinkle with the cheese and roast for about an hour until it is nice and brown (internal temperature 160°F). Cover with foil and let sit for 10-15 minutes before serving. Serves 6-8.

GROUND BEEF GRAVY
Jauhelihakastike

1 pound lean ground beef
1 onion, peeled and chopped
1 tablespoon vegetable oil or butter
1 teaspoon salt
¼ teaspoon pepper
1 teaspoon ground allspice
1 teaspoon ground paprika
3 tablespoons flour
2 cups water or beef broth
1 bay leaf
(2 tablespoons heavy cream)

In a skillet cook the chopped onion in the oil until soft and lightly browned. Add the ground beef and fry while breaking it into crumbs with a fork or a spatula. When the meat is lightly browned, add the salt, pepper, allspice, paprika and flour. Mix well and let the flour cook briefly. Add the water or beef broth, bay leaf and cream, cover and let simmer for 30 minutes. Add salt to taste. Serve with boiled potatoes or rice.

BEEF LINDSTROM
Lindströmin pihvit

This dish is very popular and probably originated in Sweden. There are several versions of it, but all use beets, potatoes and cucumber pickles. My family calls these beetburgers.

1 pound lean ground beef
2 boiled potatoes, mashed with a fork
1 onion, finely chopped
2 pickled beets, finely chopped
2 tablespoons cucumber pickles, finely chopped
1 large egg
¼ cup heavy cream
1 teaspoon salt
½ teaspoon pepper
Butter for frying
½-1 cup beef broth or water
1 tablespoon heavy cream

A food processor makes it easy to chop all the vegetables. Add the potatoes and chopped vegetables to the meat with the egg, cream, salt and pepper. Mix well. With hands dipped in cold water shape into patties and fry them in butter over low heat until nicely brown on both sides. Add ½ cup of beef broth to the pan, cover and let cook 15 minutes more. Remove to a serving dish. Rinse the pan with a little beef broth or water, add the heavy cream and pour over the patties.

MACARONI AND BEEF CASSEROLE
Lihamakaronilaatikko

2 cups elbow macaroni
1 medium onion, peeled and chopped
2 ribs celery, peeled and finely chopped
2 carrots, peeled and finely chopped

1 tablespoon vegetable oil
1 pound lean ground beef
2 teaspoons dried marjoram
1 teaspoon salt
½ teaspoon pepper
2 tablespoons butter
3 tablespoons flour
2 cups milk
6 ounces shredded pasteurized process gruyere cheese, such as Valio, or substitute Cheddar cheese
¼ teaspoon nutmeg
¼ teaspoon pepper
Salt to taste

Preheat oven to 375°F. Cook the macaroni according to package directions and drain. Turn into a buttered casserole.

In a skillet cook the onion, celery and carrots in oil until soft and lightly browned. Add the ground beef and cook until it is lightly browned, breaking it up into small crumbs with a fork or a spatula. Mix in the marjoram, salt and pepper, and let cook a few minutes more. Mix with the macaroni in the casserole.

Melt the butter in a saucepan, stir in the flour and let cook briefly. Whisk in the milk and let cook, stirring, over medium heat, for 2-3 minutes. Add the cheese and keep stirring until it melts. Add pepper, nutmeg and salt to taste. Pour over the macaroni and meat in the casserole, and bake for about 30 minutes, or until the sauce bubbles and browns on top.

MEAT PIE
Lihapiirakka

PASTRY:

2 medium boiled potatoes, peeled, mashed with fork
12 tablespoons butter or margarine (1½ sticks)
2 cups flour

Blend the butter and the flour together until the mixture resembles coarse meal. Add the potatoes and work the dough until it holds together in a ball. If necessary, add a tablespoon or two of cold water. Wrap and chill the dough for 30 minutes.

FILLING:
½ cup rice
1 cup beef broth
1 small onion, peeled and chopped
1 tablespoon butter or oil
1 pound lean ground beef
¼ pound finely chopped smoked ham
½ teaspoon salt
¼ teaspoon pepper
1 teaspoon dried marjoram leaves
4 tablespoons chopped parsley
2 hard-boiled eggs, peeled and coarsely chopped
½ cup cream or beef broth

GLAZE:
1 egg yolk
2 tablespoons milk

In a saucepan bring the rice and the beef broth to a boil, stir, cover, lower the heat and let cook for 18 minutes.

Preheat oven to 375°F. In a skillet cook the onion in butter until lightly browned. Add the meat and cook, stirring and breaking it up to small crumbs, until the meat is lightly browned. Stir in the chopped ham and cook briefly. Season with salt, pepper, marjoram and parsley. Remove from heat, stir in the rice and chopped eggs, and add enough cream or beef broth to make a fairly loose mixture. Add salt to taste.

Butter a 10-inch round cake pan or a 9x12-inch shallow baking pan. Divide the dough into two parts, one slightly bigger than the other. Roll the bigger part to cover the bottom and sides of the buttered pan and with the aid of a rolling pin transfer the dough to the pan. Spoon in the filling, roll the second part of the dough to cover the pie and turn the edges to cover the top dough. Pinch the edges together, brush with the egg yolk mixed with milk and bake for about 30 minutes, or until golden brown. Serve hot in wedges or slices, traditionally with a cup of home-made beef broth.

LAMB WITH DILL SAUCE
Tilliliha

This dish can also be made with veal or beef, using the same recipe.

2 pounds lamb, preferably from leg, cubed
Water to cover
1 teaspoon salt
1 onion, peeled and quartered
2 whole cloves
A few peppercorns
½ teaspoon whole allspice
1 bay leaf
Dill sprigs

SAUCE:
2 tablespoons butter
3 tablespoons flour
2½ cups lamb broth
1 tablespoon white vinegar
1 tablespoon sugar
3 tablespoons chopped fresh dill

Place the meat in a saucepan with water barely to cover and bring to boil over high heat. Skim off the froth as it rises to the surface. Add the salt, onion, cloves, peppercorns, allspice, bay leaf and a few dill sprigs, and simmer the meat for 1½ to 2 hours or until tender. Drain the meat, saving the broth. Keep the meat warm while you are making the sauce.

For the sauce: Melt the butter in a pan, add the flour and cook briefly. Whisk in the lamb stock and let simmer for 5 minutes. Stir in the vinegar and the sugar, and let simmer a few minutes more. Add the chopped dill, season to taste, pour over the lamb pieces and serve with new potatoes.

ROAST LEG OF LAMB
Lammaspaisti

In Finland it is customary to cook lamb until well done, but this recipe produces medium rare meat. Of course, you can increase cooking time and cook the lamb until well done, to an internal temperature of 160-170°F.

6-pound leg of lamb
1 clove garlic
1 tablespoon Dijon-style mustard
1 teaspoon dried rosemary or marjoram leaves
2 tablespoons flour
Salt, pepper
1 onion, peeled

SAUCE:
2 tablespoons butter
2 tablespoons flour
1 cup beef broth
¾ cup brewed strong coffee
1 tablespoon heavy cream

Preheat oven to 450°F. Trim all excess fat from the lamb. With a sharp pointed knife make slits into the meat near the bone and insert thin slivers of garlic. Smear the mustard all over the meat, sprinkle it with salt, pepper and the flour. Place the lamb in a roasting pan, on a rack, sprinkle it with herbs and slice the onion around it. Insert a meat thermometer in the thickest part of the meat. Roast in 450°F oven for 20 minutes, lower the heat to 350°F and roast approximately 1½ hours total roasting time, or until meat thermometer shows 140°F for medium rare. Take the roast out of the oven, place it on a hot serving platter and keep warm while you make the sauce.

In a saucepan melt the butter, add the flour and stir until light brown. Be careful not to burn the flour, take the pan off heat as soon as the flour starts to brown. Whisk in the broth, coffee and cream, and let simmer over low heat for 5 minutes. Add half a cup of water into the roasting pan, scrape up all the browned bits and strain the juices into a bowl. Skim the fat off the liquid, add it to the sauce and reheat. Season to taste and serve with the lamb. Serves 8.

VEAL CUTLET
Wieninleike

Veal cutlet Viennese style is a very popular dish in Finland and I am including it here, in order to give a representative sample of Finnish cooking. Ask your butcher to cut the veal across the grain, since this makes a more Finnish-style cutlet.

4-6 veal cutlets, pounded thin
Salt and pepper
1 large egg, lightly beaten
½ cup fine dry bread crumbs
4 tablespoons butter
4-6 slices fresh lemon
4-6 fillets of anchovies
2 teaspoons capers

Dip the pounded veal cutlets in egg and then in the bread crumbs. Sprinkle with salt and pepper. Sauté in butter in a large skillet until golden brown on both sides. Place on a serving dish and decorate each cutlet with a lemon slice, rolled anchovy fillet and a few capers.

JELLIED VEAL LOAF
Vasikanhyytelö

This can be made with veal breast or shoulder with bones included—this way using gelatine to jell the loaf is unnecessary, since veal bones have natural gelatine. A more expensive cut is veal roast; it is leaner and has less waste, but then you have to add gelatine.

2-3 pounds veal breast or shoulder, or veal roast, cut in large cubes
4 cups water, or enough to cover the meat
2 teaspoons salt
2 small onions, peeled and cut in quarters
1 bay leaf
1 teaspoon whole allspice
2 whole cloves
¼-½ cup fresh lemon juice
½ teaspoon ground ginger
1 small package gelatine
Salt to taste

Rinse the veal under cold running water, place it into a saucepan and cover it with cold water. Bring to boil and simmer for 5 minutes. Pour the water out and rinse both the saucepan and the veal with cold water. This gets rid of the froth that accumulates in the water. Put the meat back into the saucepan with enough water to barely cover it. Add the salt, onions, bay leaf, allspice and cloves. Bring to boil, cover and let simmer for 1½ to 2 hours.

Strain the broth into a bowl and let the meat cool until you can handle it. When cool, remove meat from bones and gristle and chop fine by hand or in a food processor. Return the meat into the saucepan and add enough of the broth to make a loose mixture. If there seems to be too much broth, rather than throw it away, pour it into a wide pan and reduce it over high heat to the amount that you need to make the loose mixture that you need. Add the ginger and lemon juice. Salt to taste, but you may want add a little extra salt since chilled foods need a little more flavor. Bring to boil, stirring, boil a few minutes and take off the heat. Soak the gelatine in ¼ cup of cold water until it thickens, and add into the hot veal, stirring well.

Rinse a 2-quart loaf pan with cold water and fill it with the veal mixture. Let cool, cover, and refrigerate until cold, preferably overnight. When cold and jelled, run a knife around the sides of the pan and unmold the veal onto a platter. Serve sliced, with pickled beets and cucumbers. Serves 6-8 as a main course, 10-12 buffet-style.

BOILED CHICKEN WITH CREAM SAUCE
Kanaviillokki

3½-pound chicken
Water to cover
1 onion, peeled and quartered
1 rib celery, cut in half
Pinch of thyme
1 bay leaf
¼ teaspoon whole peppercorns
1 teaspoon salt

Place the chicken into a saucepan that fits it comfortably and add enough water to just cover the chicken. Add the rest of the ingredients and bring the water to simmer, cover the pan, and let the chicken simmer until it is cooked, about 30-40 minutes. Let the chicken cool in the broth, if possible, for a more succulent taste; otherwise remove it from the broth and let cool on a plate. Peel off the skin, remove the meat from the bones and cut into serving pieces. Make the sauce and heat the chicken pieces in the sauce. Serve with rice.

SAUCE:

2 tablespoons butter
3 tablespoons flour
3 cups chicken cooking liquid
2 tablespoons heavy cream
Juice of ½ lemon
(1 teaspoon mild curry powder)
Salt to taste

Melt the butter in a saucepan and stir in the flour. Let cook briefly, then whisk in the chicken broth and the curry powder, if desired. Let simmer for 5 minutes. Stir in the cream, the lemon juice, and more salt, if needed. Add the chicken pieces into the sauce and heat until thoroughly warm.

ROAST CHICKEN
Uunissa paistettu kana

3½-pound roasting chicken
Juice of ½ lemon
½ cup fresh parsley sprigs
2 tablespoons butter
1 small onion, peeled and sliced
1 small carrot, peeled and sliced
(3 slices bacon)
Salt, pepper
½ cup chicken broth
(¼ cup heavy cream)

Preheat oven to 325°F. Rinse the chicken and pat dry with paper towels. Season the inside of the chicken with the lemon juice and insert the parsley. Truss the chicken with a piece of string. Melt the butter in a skillet and brown the chicken on all sides over medium heat until golden all over. Sprinkle the chicken with salt and pepper and place it breast up in a casserole with a lid. In the butter remaining in the skillet cook the onion and the carrot until lightly browned and add these to the casserole. Rinse the skillet with ½ cup water and pour this over the chicken. If desired, place the bacon slices across the chicken breast. Close the lid tightly and place the casserole in oven for about one hour and ten minutes. Baste the chicken occasionally. The chicken is done when the drumsticks move freely in their sockets, or insert a wooden spoon in the chicken, lift the chicken up and drain the juices from the vent. If they run clear with no trace of pink, the chicken is done. Remove the chicken to a serving plate and cover with aluminum foil to keep warm. Add the chicken broth (and the cream) to the juices in the casserole and stir to include all the brown bits in the casserole. Season with salt and pepper. Skim off the fat and strain the sauce into a sauceboat. Serve with the chicken. Roasted potatoes are often served with this dish (page 99).

LIVER AND RICE CASSEROLE
Maksalaatikko

This is one of those dishes loved by many Finns but regarded with suspicion by many foreigners. Liver casserole is a traditional Christmas dish, especially in western Finland. It is more like a stuffing and goes well with chicken or turkey. It also makes a nice dish for a smorgasbord.

½ cup rice
1 cup water
3 cups milk
1 onion, peeled and chopped
1 tablespoon butter
1 large egg
½-1 teaspoon salt
½ teaspoon pepper
3-4 tablespoons dark corn syrup or pancake syrup
½ teaspoon dried marjoram leaves

¾ pound calf's liver, ground or finely chopped in food processor
½ cup raisins

In a double boiler bring the rice and the water to boil, cover and cook for 15 minutes or until all the water is absorbed. Add the milk and cook, stirring occasionally, until thickened to a porridgelike consistency, about one hour. Let cool.

Preheat oven to 350°F. Sauté the onion in the butter until soft and lightly browned. In a bowl, mix the rice with the onion, egg, salt, pepper, syrup and marjoram. Add some more milk if necessary to make the mixture fairly loose, and more salt if needed. Add the ground liver and raisins, and mix well. Turn the mixture into an oiled casserole and bake for about an hour, or until well browned on top. Serve with lingonberries.

BRAISED LIVER
Maksakastike

1 pound calf's liver or beef liver
Flour for dredging
2 tablespoons butter
1 cup water or beef broth
½ cup half-and-half
1 tablespoon flour, preferably granulated
¼ cup water
Salt, pepper

Cut liver into thin slices and remove the membranes. Dredge it in the flour and sauté in butter, preferably in a nonstick skillet, until nicely browned on both sides. Add water or broth, cover tightly and cook over low heat for 30 minutes, or until the liver is very soft. Stir in the half-and-half and bring to boil. Mix the flour with ¼ cup water and stir into the sauce until it thickens. Simmer 5 minutes more. Season with salt and pepper. Serve with boiled potatoes.

PORK CHOPS
Porsaankyljykset

4-6 pork chops
½ cup dry bread crumbs
Salt and pepper
1 tablespoon oil
1 tablespoon butter
½ cup water
¼-½ cup cream or half-and-half

Dredge the pork chops in bread crumbs and sprinkle them with salt and pepper. Melt the oil and butter in a skillet and cook the chops until they are nicely browned on both sides. Add the water and cover the pan tightly. Let the chops cook on low heat until tender, about 45 minutes. Remove to a serving dish, add the cream to the skillet, raise the heat and cook the sauce until thickened. Pour over the chops and serve.

PORK GRAVY
Sianlihakastike

This is another traditional Finnish dish that together with boiled potatoes was the mainstay of many kitchens in earlier times. The fresh side of pork used for this dish is not readily available here, as most of it is smoked for bacon or salted for salt pork. The dish can be made with meaty salt pork or bacon, but sliced loin with a little fat attached is a very good substitute.

¾ pound thinly sliced pork
1 small onion, peeled and chopped
4 tablespoons flour
2-3 cups water
(¾ teaspoon salt)
(1 teaspoon mustard)

In a skillet over medium heat fry the pork slices until nicely browned. Add the chopped onion and cook until lightly browned. Move the meat slices to the side of the pan and stir in the flour to the drippings, cooking and stirring until the flour is lightly browned. Add the water and the salt, if you didn't use salt pork, and stir until the gravy is smooth. Cover and let simmer for 30-45 minutes, until the meat is tender and the gravy is smooth. Salt to taste and season with mustard, if desired. Serve with boiled potatoes.

If you use bacon for this dish, add milk instead of water to the gravy.

HAM PANCAKE
Kinkkupannukakku

Serve this with a green salad for lunch, or cut it into small squares for an appetizer.

3 cups milk
1½ cups flour, preferably granulated
2 medium onions, peeled and chopped
1 tablespoon butter
½ pound chopped smoked ham
3 large eggs
¼ teaspoon salt

In a bowl stir the milk gradually into the flour. Let the batter rest for 30 minutes. Preheat oven to 400°F. In a skillet cook the onions in butter until soft and lightly browned. Add the ham and cook until lightly browned. Beat the eggs into the batter and add the ham along with the sautéed onions and the salt. Pour the batter into a buttered 9x12-inch baking pan and bake for about 30 minutes, or until puffed and browned. Let the pancake cool for 3-4 minutes before you cut it into big squares to serve.

FINNISH HASH
Pyttipannu

This is originally a Swedish dish and is a very popular way to use leftover beef and ham.

4 cups raw potatoes, peeled and cut into small dice
2 tablespoons oil
2 tablespoons butter
2 medium onions, peeled and chopped
3 cups cooked beef or ham, or a combination of the two, cut into small dice
Salt and pepper to taste
4-6 eggs
1 tablespoon chopped parsley

After dicing the potatoes, keep them in cold water to prevent discoloration. Drain the potatoes and pat them dry in paper towels. Brown them over medium heat in half the butter and oil in a preferably nonstick skillet. Stir and shake the pan often to get them to brown evenly. When cooked, remove the potatoes to a dish and keep warm.

In the same skillet cook the onion in the rest of the butter and oil, until it is soft and lightly browned. Add the meats and brown them on all sides, stirring and shaking the pan to get an even result. Return the cooked potatoes into the pan and stir to mix well. Sprinkle with salt and pepper to taste. Transfer to a serving dish or individual plates and keep warm.

In the same skillet, cook the eggs only on one side, so that the yolk acts as a sauce for the hash. Serve the hash with the egg on top, sprinkled with parsley.

CHRISTMAS HAM
Joulukinkku

Although recently turkey has made inroads into the Finnish Christmas, ham is still the overwhelming favorite for Christmas Eve dinner.

In the old days, when hams were stored in salt brine, the hams were first soaked and boiled to reduce saltiness. After that, the ham was tightly covered with a dough made with water and rye flour, to preserve the juiciness, and baked in the oven for hours until tender. Finally, the rye dough covering was removed, the ham was sprinkled with bread crumbs and cooked in the oven until the bread crumbs were browned.

This recipe is for the smoked ham commonly found is supermarkets. A 16-pound ham is quite large for most households, but it serves a number of friends and relatives, who gather for Christmas dinner, with plenty of leftovers for soups and sandwiches. Of course you can cook half a ham or one of the boned hams instead.

16-pound fully cooked smoked ham
3 tablespoons brown sugar
3 tablespoons prepared mustard
Whole cloves for decorating
1 cup dry bread crumbs

Preheat oven to 325°F. Rinse the ham and place it fat side up on a rack in a roasting pan. Place the pan in the oven and count for a cooking time about ½ hour per pound, depending on the shape of the ham and your oven. It can take anywhere from 6 to 8 hours to reach an internal temperature of 160°F. When the ham is almost done, remove it from the oven, cut off the skin and all the visible fat and discard. Mix the brown sugar with the mustard and spread all over the ham. With a sharp knife score the ham in a diamond pattern, insert a whole clove into every diamond and sprinkle bread crumbs all over the ham. Return the ham to the oven and cook until the bread crumbs are nicely browned. Remove the ham to a serving dish and serve either warm or cold.

VORSCHMACK

General Mannerheim was the Commander-in-Chief in the Finnish Winter War and the Continuation War in the years 1939-1944. He was also the President of Finland 1944-1946. He was a very well-educated man; he spoke many languages fluently and served the Czar in St. Petersburg before Finland became independent. He enjoyed good food, and especially ordinary dishes, well prepared. This dish was one of his favorites, and it is still served in Finland at the restaurant he used to frequent. This is a slightly modified version of the dish.

2 pounds lamb, from leg or shoulder, cubed
½ pound stewing beef
2 medium onions, peeled and quartered
1 fillet of salt herring, soaked for 24 hours and rinsed
1 3½-ounce can of Swedish anchovies
2 cloves garlic
Pepper

Preheat oven to 450°F. Place the meats and onions into a roasting pan and roast them until browned and well done. Let cool slightly. Using a food processor or a meat grinder, grind the meats and onions along with the herring, anchovies and garlic. Turn the mixture into a saucepan, add the liquid from the baking pan and pepper to taste. Heat the mixture to boiling, lower the heat, cover and let simmer for 30 minutes to an hour. If the mixture seems too dry, add some beef broth, heavy cream or sour cream. Traditionally *vorschmack* is served with sour cream, baked potatoes and beer.

IV.

VEGETABLES AND SIDE DISHES

NEW POTATOES WITH ONION AND BUTTER SAUCE

Uudet perunat sipuli-voikastikkeen kera

Use the small tender new potatoes that need no peeling, only scrubbing. Slightly older ones need to be cut in half but left unpeeled.

1 pound new potatoes
2 tablespoons butter
1 small onion, sliced or 2 tablespoons chopped fresh chives
2 tablespoons water
Salt to taste

Boil the potatoes until tender when pierced with a fork, 15-20 minutes. Drain. In a small saucepan bring the butter, water and onion or chives to boil and let simmer over very low heat for 5 minutes. Add salt to taste. Pour over the hot potatoes.

MASHED POTATOES

Perunasose

7 cups peeled potatoes, cut in chunks
1 teaspoon salt
¼ teaspoon ground nutmeg
2 cups hot milk

In a saucepan, cook the potatoes in salted water to cover until they can be pierced easily with a fork. Drain the potatoes and leave them uncovered for a couple of minutes to let the steam escape. Place them in a bowl and beat with an electric mixer on medium speed until smooth. Add the nutmeg and gradually beat in the hot milk until you reach the desired consistency. Beat in salt to taste. Serves 6-8.

SAUTÉED POTATOES WITH ONION

Paistetut sipuliperunat

6 medium potatoes
2 medium onions
1 tablespoon vegetable oil
1 small garlic clove
Salt and pepper to taste

Peel and slice the potatoes and onions. In a nonstick skillet, heat the oil and sauté the minced garlic for a few seconds. Add the potatoes and onions and sauté on medium low heat, stirring and turning the potatoes occasionally with a spatula until the potatoes are nicely browned and soft, about 45 minutes. Add salt and freshly ground pepper to taste.

OVEN ROASTED POTATOES

Uunissa paistetut perunat

6-8 medium potatoes
1 large onion
1 tablespoon vegetable oil
½ cup beef or chicken broth, or water
Salt and pepper to taste

Preheat oven to 375°F. Peel the potatoes and halve them lengthwise. Cut each half into 3-4 wedges. Do the same with the onion. In a roasting pan mix the onions and the potatoes with the vegetable oil and roast the potatoes, stirring frequently, for about 2 hours, or until nicely browned. If potatoes start to stick onto the roasting pan, pour in some broth or water and scrape them loose. Sprinkle the potatoes with salt and pepper to taste while they are roasting.

CREAMED POTATOES
Maitoperunamuhennos

6 medium potatoes
1 tablespoon vegetable oil
1 tablespoon butter
2 cups milk
1 teaspoon salt
¼ teaspoon pepper
Chopped parsley or chives

Peel the potatoes and cut them into ½-inch dice. Rinse them well in cold water and pat dry on paper towels. In a nonstick skillet melt the butter with the oil and stir the potatoes until they are coated with butter, but do not let them take color. Add the milk and cook the potatoes, partially covered, over low heat, stirring often, until they are soft and have absorbed the milk, about 30-40 minutes. Mix in salt and pepper to taste and sprinkle with the chopped parsley or chives.

MASHED POTATO CASSEROLE
Perunalaatikko

1½ quarts peeled potatoes, cut in chunks
2 cups hot milk
1 tablespoon butter
2 tablespoons flour
1 teaspoon salt
1 tablespoon dark corn syrup or pancake syrup
¼ teaspoon ground nutmeg

Boil the potatoes in water until tender. Drain well. Preheat oven to 275°F. Mash the potatoes with an electric mixer, and gradually stir in the hot milk, butter, flour, salt, syrup and nutmeg. Turn into a buttered 2-quart casserole that is high enough to allow the potatoes to swell up. Bake in 275°F oven for 3-4 hours, until nicely browned on top.

RUTABAGA CASSEROLE
Lanttulaatikko

2 medium rutabagas
1 teaspoon salt
1 tablespoon butter
2 tablespoons dark corn syrup or pancake syrup
1 tablespoon flour
¼ teaspoon white pepper
1 cup milk or cream
1 large egg
¼ cup dry bread crumbs

Peel and cut the rutabagas in 1-inch cubes, and put them into a stainless steel or enameled saucepan. Pour in enough water to barely cover the vegetables and add the salt. Bring to boil, lower the heat and simmer for 20-30 minutes, or until tender when tested with a fork.

Preheat oven to 350°F. Drain the rutabagas and mash them using a potato masher, an electric mixer or a food processor. Add the butter, syrup, flour and pepper. Stir in enough milk or cream to make a fairly loose mixture. Add salt to taste. When somewhat cooled, beat in the egg. Pour into a buttered casserole and sprinkle the top with the bread crumbs. Bake for 1 hour or until nicely browned on top. Serve hot.

BROWNED RUTABAGAS
Paistetut lantut

During the long winter in the old days, when fresh vegetables were not available, root vegetables were stored in cellars, and they were used instead. This rutabaga dish was often served with a pot roast or other dishes made with beef.

1 small rutabaga
2 tablespoons butter
2 teaspoons brown sugar or pancake syrup
Salt and pepper to taste

Peel the rutabaga and cut it into small cubes, about ½ inch in diameter. In a heavy skillet melt the butter and sauté the cubes over medium heat until brown on all sides, stirring often. Add the sugar or the syrup, cover and let cook over low heat, stirring occasionally, for 20-30 minutes, or until soft. Add salt and pepper to taste.

CARROT AND RICE CASSEROLE
Porkkanalaatikko

½ cup rice
1 cup water
3 cups milk
4 cups finely shredded carrots
1 teaspoon salt
2 tablespoons dark corn syrup or pancake syrup
⅛ teaspoon pepper
⅛ teaspoon ground ginger
1 large egg
2 tablespoons dry bread crumbs

On top of a double boiler over simmering water cook the rice in the water for about 15 minutes, or until all the water is absorbed. Add 2 cups milk, cover and cook, stirring occasionally, until the mixture thickens to a porridge, about 45 minutes. Let cool to lukewarm.

Preheat oven to 350°F. Stir the carrots, salt, syrup, pepper, ginger and rest of the milk into the rice, and add the lightly beaten egg.

Turn the mixture into a buttered casserole, sprinkle the top with the bread crumbs and bake the casserole for an hour, or until nicely browned on top.

CREAMED SPINACH
Pinaattimuhennos

1 pound fresh spinach or 1 package (10 ounces) frozen spinach
1 tablespoon butter
2 tablespoons flour
1 cup milk, or half cream and half milk
Salt and pepper to taste
Small pinch ground cloves

Wash the spinach well in several changes of water to remove all sand, and blanche it in boiling water for a few minutes, until wilted. Cook frozen spinach according to package directions. Drain and squeeze the spinach dry and chop it finely, if desired. In a saucepan, melt the butter and cook the flour in it briefly. Whisk in the milk, or milk and cream, and stir until thickened. Add the spinach and mix well. Season with salt, pepper, and a very small pinch of cloves.

SPINACH PANCAKES
Pinaattiohukaiset

2 cups milk
1 cup flour
3/4 teaspoon salt
2 large eggs
3/4 pound fresh spinach, rinsed, blanched, squeezed dry and finely chopped, or 1 package chopped frozen spinach, cooked, squeezed dry and finely chopped
1/8 teaspoon pepper

¼ teaspoon ground nutmeg
Small pinch cloves
2 tablespoons melted butter

In a bowl or electric blender, mix the milk with the flour and salt. Let sit for about an hour to allow the mixture to thicken slightly. If you don't have time to wait, add ¼ cup more flour to make the batter easier to handle. Beat in the eggs and add the chopped spinach, seasonings, and melted butter.

Heat a Scandinavian plett pan or a 10-12 inch skillet. If you use a nonstick pan, you don't have to grease it; otherwise grease it lightly for the first batch. Drop about 2 tablespoons of the batter into the pan and spread it out with a spatula to make a round pancake. Fill the skillet with pancakes, and cook them 1-2 minutes on each side, until they have browned lightly. Keep warm while finishing the rest of the pancakes. Serve as a vegetable course or a light luncheon dish, accompanied by lingonberries.

CREAMED MUSHROOMS
Sienimuhennos

The most common way Finns cook their wild mushrooms is in this very simple stew, which is delicious with boiled new potatoes, meat loaf or sautéed fish. A little bit of white wine or white vermouth added to the mushrooms adds a nice flavor.

4 cups sliced fresh mushrooms
2 tablespoons butter
1 medium onion, peeled and finely chopped
2 tablespoons flour
1½ cups milk or cream
Salt and pepper to taste

Melt the butter in a large skillet. Cook the onion until it is translucent, add the mushrooms and cook, stirring, over high heat, until the mushrooms are dry and lightly browned. Mix in the flour and cook briefly, then add the milk and stir until thickened. Cover, and let cook over low heat, stirring occasionally, for 15 minutes, adding more milk if necessary. Add salt and pepper to taste. For festive occasions, use cream instead of milk.

BAKED CAULIFLOWER
Kuorrutettu kukkakaali

1 large cauliflower
Salt

SAUCE:
2 tablespoons butter
3 tablespoons flour
2 cups milk
½ teaspoon salt
White pepper
1 cup grated Finland Swiss cheese

Preheat oven to 375°F. Rinse, trim and separate the cauliflower into florets. Cook in boiling salted water for 10 minutes and drain. For the sauce, melt the butter in a saucepan, stir in the flour and let cook briefly. Add the milk and beat with a whisk until sauce thickens and becomes smooth. Season with salt and pepper. Place the cauliflower into a buttered baking dish, pour the sauce over, and sprinkle with the cheese. Bake until the cheese has melted and lightly browned.

BRAISED RED CABBAGE
Haudutettu punakaali

1 red cabbage, coarsely shredded
2 tablespoons oil or butter
1 large onion, peeled and chopped

2 apples, peeled, cored and chopped
¼ teaspoon pepper
¼ teaspoon ground cloves
⅓ cup dark corn syrup or pancake syrup
2 tablespoons white vinegar
½ teaspoon salt, or to taste

In a 4-quart casserole brown the chopped onion in the oil or butter. Add the shredded cabbage, apples and seasonings, and mix well. Cover and let cook over medium heat about one hour, stirring occasionally. Towards the end of the cooking time, remove the cover, raise the heat and let most of the liquid in the casserole boil away, stirring often.

CABBAGE PIE
Kaalipiirakka

PASTRY:

1 cup butter or margarine (2 sticks)
2½ cups flour
½ teaspoon salt
2 medium boiled potatoes, peeled and mashed with a fork
2-3 tablespoons cold water

Blend the flour with the butter and salt until the mixture resembles a meal. Add the potatoes and enough cold water to form a dough. Refrigerate while you are making the filling.

FILLING:

1 large head of cabbage, core removed and thinly shredded
3 tablespoons butter
1 teaspoon salt
½ teaspoon pepper
2 tablespoons dark corn syrup or pancake syrup

GLAZE:
1 egg yolk
2 tablespoons milk

In a 10-12-inch skillet melt the butter and add the cabbage. Cook over medium heat, stirring often, until cabbage is soft and lightly browned. Stir in salt, pepper and syrup. Let cool.

Assembly: Preheat oven to 400°F. Spread parchment paper the size of your baking sheet on a slightly dampened surface. On it, roll the dough with a rolling pin into a square about ½ inch thick. Lift the parchment paper with the dough on it onto a baking sheet. Spread the filling on half of the dough and lift the other half over the filling and tuck under the bottom dough. Seal the ends by tucking them under. Score lightly with the tines of a fork for decoration, baste with an egg glaze (the egg yolk beaten with the milk) and bake for 30 minutes, or until nicely browned. Serve hot, with sour cream.

MACARONI PUDDING
Makaronilaatikko

This casserole is often served as a side dish with meatballs, or as a meatless main dish with a nice salad on the side.

2 cups elbow macaroni
3 cups milk
3 large eggs
¾ teaspoon salt
¼ teaspoon pepper
1 teaspoon sugar
¼ teaspoon ground nutmeg
1 cup grated Swiss cheese

Boil the macaroni in salted water according to package directions and drain well. Turn into a buttered 2-quart casserole. Preheat the oven to 350°F. In a bowl whisk the eggs with 1 cup of the milk until thoroughly mixed, add the rest of the milk and the sugar, salt, pepper, and the nutmeg. Pour over the macaroni. The liquid should just barely cover the macaroni; if needed, add some more milk. Sprinkle the top with the grated cheese and bake for about one hour, or until firm and nicely browned on top.

V.

APPETIZERS, SALADS AND SANDWICHES

HERRING SALAD
Kermasilli

1 12-ounce jar of herring fillets in wine sauce, drained and chopped into ½-inch pieces, or a small salt herring, soaked for 24 hours, rinsed, filleted, and chopped
⅓ cup heavy cream, lightly whipped
1 teaspoon white vinegar
1 teaspoon sugar
¼ cup finely chopped chives or onion
¼ cup chopped fresh dill
2 hard-boiled eggs, chopped

Mix the heavy cream, vinegar and sugar, and fold in the herring, chives or onion, and dill. Turn into a serving dish and garnish with the chopped egg.

GLASSBLOWER'S HERRING
Lasimestarin silli

2 salted herring or 4 fillets of matjes herring
½ cup white vinegar
½ cup water
½ cup sugar
1 teaspoon whole black pepper
1 teaspoon whole allspice
2 teaspoons whole mustard seeds
2 bay leaves
1 medium red onion or yellow onion, peeled and sliced
1 carrot, peeled and sliced
1-inch piece of fresh horseradish root, scraped and grated or 2 tablespoons prepared horseradish

Clean the salt herring, fillet them and soak them in cold water for 24 hours. Heat the vinegar with the water and the sugar, pepper, allspice, bay leaves and mustard seeds in a stainless steel or enameled pan until the sugar has completely dissolved. Let cool to room temperature. Rinse the herring, and slice them in 1-inch pieces.

Layer the herring pieces with the onion, carrot and horseradish into a glass jar, about 1 quart in size, and pour some of the vinegar mixture over every layer. When finished, the vinegar should just cover the contents. Cover the jar and refrigerate for 2-3 days. Serve as an appetizer with hot boiled potatoes, or as a part of a smorgasbord.

DEVILED EGGS
Täytetyt munat

6 hard-boiled eggs
2-3 tablespoons mayonnaise or heavy cream
¼-½ teaspoon salt
½-1 teaspoon mild curry powder, or to taste
Paprika for sprinkling

Halve the hard-boiled eggs lengthwise and remove the yolks into a bowl. Mix in salt and curry powder to taste, and enough cream or mayonnaise to make a smooth paste. Fill the egg halves with the paste, either using a spoon, or use a pastry bag to pipe the filling in the egg halves. Sprinkle with paprika for color.

The eggs can additionally be decorated several different ways: parsley sprigs, dill sprigs, sliced olives, tiny shrimp, small pieces of ham, asparagus tips, small pieces of herring, all according to your taste.

LIVER PATÉ
Maksapasteija

1 pound calf's liver
2 large eggs
1 small onion, peeled and quartered

3 fillets of Swedish anchovies
1 tablespoon brine from the can of anchovies
¼ cup flour
¾ cup heavy cream
½ teaspoon dried marjoram, crumbled
½ teaspoon ground ginger
½ teaspoon ground allspice
½ teaspoon ground pepper
1 teaspoon salt

Preheat oven to 350°F. Remove the membranes from the liver and cut it into small pieces. Place the eggs into the bowl of a food processor or a blender, and process for a few seconds. Add the onion and process a few seconds more. Add the liver and the anchovies, and the rest of the ingredients and process until you get a smooth mixture. Butter a loaf pan and line it with parchment paper. Pour in the mixture, cover the pan with aluminum foil and set it into a bigger pan of hot water. Bake in the oven for 2-2½ hours, or until set, and a knife plunged into the middle comes out clean. Cool and unmold onto a serving dish. Keep refrigerated until ready to serve.

OLD FASHIONED LETTUCE SALAD
Vanhanajan lehtisalaatti

1 large head Boston lettuce
1 hard-boiled egg, white and yolk separated
1 tablespoon white vinegar
1 teaspoon sugar
1 teaspoon mustard
Pinch of salt
¼ cup heavy cream

Wash the lettuce well and dry the leaves. In a large bowl mix the cooked, crumbled egg yolk with the vinegar, sugar, mustard and salt. Whisk in the cream with a wire whip until the mixture thickens lightly. Add the coarsely torn leaves of lettuce, and mix to coat the leaves. Sprinkle with chopped egg white before serving.

TOMATO AND ONION SALAD
Tomaatti-sipulisalaatti

4 medium tomatoes
1 medium onion, peeled and thinly sliced
4 tablespoons oil and vinegar dressing
Fresh dill sprigs

Chop the tomatoes in coarse chunks and peel and slice the onion. Combine with the dressing and chill for about an hour before serving. Decorate with fresh dill.

OIL AND VINEGAR DRESSING
Öljykastike

1 tablespoon wine vinegar
3 tablespoons oil
¼ teaspoon sugar
Pinch of salt and pepper

Beat all ingredients together and pour over the tomatoes.

CUCUMBER SALAD
Kurkkusalaatti

½ seedless European style cucumber
½ teaspoon salt
1 tablespoon sugar
2 tablespoons white vinegar
1 tablespoon chopped fresh dill

Wash and thinly slice the cucumber. Place the slices on a plate, sprinkle with salt, sugar and the chopped dill. Cover with another plate inverted over the first one, and shake the cucumbers a couple of minutes until they release some of their juices. Sprinkle with the vinegar, cover with a plastic wrap and refrigerate for at least 30 minutes before serving.

CUCUMBER AND ONION SALAD
Kurkku-sipulisalaatti

1 pound small cucumbers (3-4 medium)
1 big yellow onion
1 cup sugar
⅓ cup white vinegar
1½ teaspoons salt
1 teaspoon dry mustard
¼ cup chopped fresh dill

Wash the cucumbers well with a brush and slice off both ends. Peel the onion and shred the onion and the cucumbers into a bowl. In a stainless steel or enameled saucepan boil the vinegar together with the sugar, salt and mustard until the sugar has dissolved. Pour over the cucumber mixture in the bowl, add the chopped dill, and mix well. The liquid should just cover the cucumbers. Cover the bowl with plastic wrap and refrigerate for 24 to 48 hours. Drain the salad in a sieve and serve as a condiment with meats and poultry. Goes especially well with hamburgers.

MUSHROOM SALAD
Sienisalaatti

1 pound mushrooms
1 tablespoon lemon juice
2 tablespoons grated onion

¼ cup heavy cream, lightly whipped
¼ cup sour cream or plain yogurt
2 tablespoons wine vinegar
2 teaspoons sugar
Salt and pepper to taste

Trim the stem ends, wash and slice the mushrooms. In a stainless steel or enameled saucepan bring 1 cup water to boil with the lemon juice. Toss in the sliced mushrooms, cover the pan, and boil briefly, 1-2 minutes. Drain well and let cool. Combine the cream, the sour cream or yogurt, vinegar, sugar, salt, and pepper. Add the mushrooms and the onion, and mix well. Line a bowl with lettuce leaves and mound the mushrooms in the center. In Finland this salad is often served with boiled potatoes and dark sour rye bread as a light meal in itself.

CHEESE AND RADISH SALAD
Juustoretiisisalaatti

This salad makes nice sandwiches spooned into small split rolls.

½ pound Finland Swiss cheese
1 bunch red radishes
2 tablespoons finely chopped parsley

DRESSING:
¼ cup mayonnaise
¼ cup sour cream
1 teaspoon Dijon-type mustard
Salt and pepper to taste

Coarsely shred the cheese and radishes in a food processor, or finely chop them by hand. Mix the dressing ingredients and combine with the cheese, radishes and parsley. Chill before serving.

CABBAGE AND LINGONBERRY SALAD
Kaali-puolukkasalaatti

4 cups finely shredded cabbage
3-4 tablespoons lingonberries stirred with sugar, or substitute whole cranberry sauce

Mix the ingredients together well and chill. This salad is especially good with meats and poultry.

CABBAGE SALAD
Kaalisalaatti

1 small head cabbage, finely shredded
2 carrots, finely shredded
Salt and pepper

DRESSING:
2 tablespoons mayonnaise
2 tablespoons white vinegar
1 tablespoon sugar

Mix shredded cabbage and carrots in a large bowl. Season with salt and pepper to taste. Mix dressing ingredients and stir into the cabbage mixture. Chill for 30 minutes before serving.

POTATO SALAD WITH DILL
Perunasalaatti

2 pounds boiling potatoes, scrubbed
4 tablespoons vegetable oil
2 tablespoons white vinegar
1 teaspoon Dijon-style mustard
2 tablespoons chopped fresh dill
Salt and pepper to taste

Boil the potatoes in their jackets until they can be easily pierced with a fork. Drain, cool, peel and slice the potatoes. Sprinkle with salt and pepper to taste. Combine the oil with the vinegar and mustard, and gently mix with the potatoes along with the dill. Refrigerate for at least an hour before serving.

BEET SALAD
Sallatti or rosolli

This is another Finnish dish that is indispensable on Finnish festive tables. It is served on every Christmas table and smorgardsbord. On Midsummer tables it is often the main dish along with some chilled cooked fish and a dessert of a custardy oven pancake. In western Finland it is called sallatti; with the addition of chopped salt herring it is called sillisalaatti or rosolli.

4 cups boiled chopped freshly cooked or canned beets
2 cups cooked chopped carrots
2 cups boiled chopped potatoes
½ cup chopped cucumber pickles
(¼ cup finely chopped onion)
(¼ cup chopped salt herring)
Salt to taste

DRESSING:
2 tablespoons mayonnaise and 2 tablespoons heavy cream or 4 tablespoons heavy cream, lightly whipped
2 tablespoons white vinegar
2 tablespoons sugar
(1 hard-boiled egg, chopped)

In a small bowl mix all the dressing ingredients together. In another bowl, mix the salad vegetables carefully together and add salt to taste. If you are using salt herring, you need less salt. Fold in the dressing well and let the salad chill in the refrigerator for a couple of hours before serving. You may decorate the salad with chopped egg before serving.

You may also serve the salad and the dressing separately; in that case use some of the beet cooking water to color the dressing pink.

COOKED VEGETABLE SALAD
Italian salaatti

In Finland this is called Italian salad, and I prefer not to try guessing why. Cooked vegetables and meats in mayonnaise-based dressing certainly do not appear to be something eaten in Italy. Nevertheless, it is a popular salad in Finland.

3 medium boiled potatoes, peeled and chopped
3 medium cooked carrots, peeled and chopped
1 medium Golden Delicious or Granny Smith apple, chopped
½ cup chopped dill pickles
1 cup cooked green peas
1 cup chopped cooked ham

DRESSING:
¼ cup mayonnaise
¼ cup sour cream or heavy cream
1 tablespoon wine vinegar
Salt and pepper to taste

Mix the dressing ingredients in a large bowl. Add the chopped vegetables and the ham and mix well. Chill before serving.

SMOKED HAM SALAD
Kinkkusalaatti

This salad makes a nice addition to a smorgasbord, but can also be used to make a sandwich.

1 cup smoked cooked ham, chopped into pea-size pieces
2 medium Golden Delicious or Granny Smith apples, chopped into pea-size pieces
2 cups cooked peas
1 teaspoon finely minced onion
1 tablespoon finely chopped parsley
Salt and pepper to taste

DRESSING:
½ cup mayonnaise
¼ cup sour cream
Salt and pepper to taste

Mix all the salad ingredients and add just enough dressing to coat the ingredients lightly. Add pepper and salt if needed. Chill before serving.

PICKLED BEETS
Etikkapunajuuret

2 cups sliced freshly cooked or canned beets
¼ cup white vinegar
¼ cup water
¼ cup sugar
½ teaspoon salt
2 whole cloves

In a stainless steel or enameled saucepan briefly boil the vinegar, water, sugar, salt and cloves. Pour over the beets in a glass, enameled or stainless steel bowl. Let cool, cover and refrigerate for a few hours before serving.

PICKLED PUMPKIN
Kurpitsasalaatti

3-4 cups peeled pumpkin, seeds and membranes removed, cut into $^3/_4$ -inch cubes
1 cup white vinegar
1 cup sugar
1 cup water
1 stick cinnamon
10 whole cloves
$^1/_2$ teaspoon whole white peppercorns

Combine the vinegar, sugar and water in a stainless steel or enameled saucepan. Bring to boil, and stir until the sugar has dissolved. Simmer for 5 minutes. Tie the spices in a rinsed cheesecloth and add to the saucepan along with the pumpkin cubes. Bring to boil, reduce heat, cover, and simmer until pumpkin is soft and almost transparent, about one hour. Remove the spices, let pumpkin cool in the liquid and chill before serving.

KARELIAN RYE PASTRIES
Karjalanpiirakat

These filled rye pastries were originally from Karelia, but have become very popular all over Finland. They are often eaten as an accompaniment to coffee or tea, or as a small snack in the evening or after the sauna. They are sold in bakeries, coffee shops and snack bars all over Finland. The pastries are made either with rice or potato filling, rice being the more popular one, and are most often accompanied by butter which is flavored with hard-boiled eggs.

CRUST:

1 cup water
1 teaspoon salt
2 cups rye flour
1 cup all-purpose flour

RICE FILLING:

1 cup rice
2 cups water
3 cups milk
1 teaspoon salt

POTATO FILLING:

1½ quarts peeled potatoes, cut in chunks
water, salt
1 cup hot milk
2 tablespoons butter
2 eggs
1 teaspoon salt

GLAZE:

1 cup milk
¼ cup butter

EGG BUTTER:

½ cup butter, softened
2 hard-boiled eggs
Salt to taste

Start by making the filling. For rice filling, bring the rice to boil with the water, cover, lower the heat and simmer until all the water is absorbed, about 18 minutes. Add the milk, and simmer, stirring often, until thickened and rice grains are very soft, about one hour. Season with salt. Let cool.

To make potato filling: Boil the potatoes with water to cover until done. Drain the water well, mash the potatoes with a mixer, add the hot milk and the butter, and salt to taste. Let cool. When cool, add the eggs and mix well.

To make the pastries: Preheat oven to 450°F. Combine the flours and the salt and add enough water to make a stiff but pliable dough. On a floured board shape the dough into a long strand and cut the strand into about 20 small pieces. Shape the pieces into small balls, flatten them, and with a rolling pin roll into thin rounds, about 6 inches in diameter. As you are making the rounds, stack them, sprinkling liberally with rye flour in between the rounds. Take the rounds, one by one, and add 1 heaping tablespoon of the filling in the middle. Spread the filling, leaving about one inch of the dough visible. Bring the sides of the dough to the center, leaving about 1 inch of the filling exposed, and crimp the edges of the dough with fingers, as for a pie, to make an oval boat-shaped pastry. Bake the pastries on a baking sheet lined with parchment paper, or lightly greased, for about 15 minutes, until lightly browned.

For glaze, melt the butter with the milk in a small skillet, and one by one dip the pastries into the milk as they come from the oven, making sure that all the surfaces are wetted. Stack them in a casserole and keep the casserole tightly covered to soften the pastries. Serve warm, with a tablespoon of egg butter.

To make egg butter: Soften the butter and mix well with finely chopped hard-boiled eggs. Add salt to taste.

BLINIS
Blinit

Blinis are a traditional Lenten dish from Russia. They are served with melted butter, sour cream, and often with chopped onions and caviar or salted fish roe. They are usually served as an appetizer or as a lunch dish, or an evening snack.

2 cups milk
¼ cup warm water (110°F)
1 envelope dry yeast
1 cup buckwheat flour
1 teaspoon salt
½ cup heavy cream or sour cream
1 cup flour
2 large eggs, separated
2 tablespoons butter, melted

In a saucepan, heat 1 cup of milk until small bubbles form on the side of the pan and let cool to lukewarm. Dissolve the yeast in the warm water and add to the milk. Whisk in the buckwheat flour. Cover with a plastic wrap and let rise in a warm place for 2 hours. At this point, you may refrigerate the dough overnight. Bring back to room temperature before continuing with the recipe.

Warm the rest of the milk to lukewarm and beat it into the batter with the salt, cream, flour and egg yolks. Cover the bowl with plastic wrap and let rise again for about an hour, until bubbly and double in bulk. Beat the egg whites until hard peaks are formed when the beater is lifted. Fold the egg whites gently but thoroughly into the batter along with the melted butter.

Blinis are traditionally cooked in special blini pans, but you may use a Scandinavian plett pan or a large, preferably nonstick skillet. Heat the skillet, and with a tablespoon drop mounds of the batter on the greased pan. Let cook over moderate heat until the edges seem cooked through, turn over and brown the other side. Keep pancakes hot in the oven while you are cooking the rest of the batter. Serve the pancakes hot.

FRESH EGG CHEESE
Munajuusto

Finns still often make this kind of cheese at home for special occasions. In summer, at marketplaces around the country, farmers still bring their own homemade cheeses for sale. This one is very easy to make and can be served on a smorgasbord, or for coffee. Finely chopped herbs can be added for flavor, if the cheese is to be served within a couple of days. The cheese also makes a nice dessert served with fruits or berries, or with a strawberry sauce.

3 large eggs
1 quart buttermilk
1 cup sour cream
3 quarts milk
1 teaspoon sugar
1 teaspoon salt

Beat the eggs with the sour cream and the buttermilk. Heat the milk to a boiling point, but do not let boil. Beat the buttermilk mixture into the milk. Bring again to boiling point and remove from heat. Let stand until the milk curdles and you can see milk solids in the mixture, about one hour. Drain the mixture through a fine sieve lined with a cheesecloth. Line a cheese mold or a root basket with a well-worn clean kitchen towel or several thicknesses of cheesecloth and set the mold on a rack over a plate. Pack the cheese firmly into the mold and sprinkle salt and a little sugar between the layers of cheese. Bring the sides of the towel up over the cheese and put a plate with a can of food over the cheese for weight. Let drain in refrigerator overnight. Unmold and remove the cheesecloth to serve.

MILK CHEESE
Maitojuusto

This cheese can also be made with skim milk.

4 quarts milk
¼ of a rennet tablet (available at pharmacies)
4 teaspoons salt

Dissolve the rennet tablet in ¼ cup of water. You will have to break it up with a back of a spoon to help it dissolve. In a stainless steel 5-quart saucepan heat the milk over low heat to 90-95°F. Remove the pot from heat and whisk in the salt and the dissolved rennet. Place the pot in a warm place, cover it with lid and kitchen towels and let it stand undisturbed for 2½-3 hours. The stainless steel saucepan will hold heat better than any other kind of pot. If you don't have a stainless pan that big, use another kind of saucepan, but keep it warm in kitchen sink in 90°F water. Check the formation of curds by drawing a spoon in the middle: the milk should look like yogurt, the curds should separate easily from the whey.

Take a long knife and slice the curds at ½-inch intervals, criss-crossing the surface and tilting the knife to slice the curds also horizontally. If the curds do not separate easily, heat the mixture slightly, and wait another 5 minutes. Place a colander in the sink, line it with a damp doubled-up cheesecloth or a well worn clean kitchen towel, and pour the contents of the pot through it. Let the curds drain for an hour, then take all four corners of the cheesecloth and knot them together. Lift the curd package up and hang over the kitchen sink from the kitchen faucet, making sure that the bottom of the package does not touch the sink. You can also hang it from a wooden spoon over the cooking pot; just make sure you keep emptying the whey as it accumulates. Let drain for 1 hour.

If you have a cheese mold, transfer the curds into that; if not, take an 8 or 9-inch cake pan with a removable bottom. Roll some aluminum foil into a strip a few layers thick, and cut the strip into four pieces. Place the pieces between the rim and the bottom of the cake pan, leaving enough room for the liquids to drain through the resulting cracks. Place the cake pan onto a rack on a plate and transfer the cheese in the cheesecloth to the cake pan. Open the cheesecloth and with a spoon pack the curds all around the pan. Taste for salt, and if necessary, sprinkle some on the curds. Fold the sides of the cheesecloth back on the curds and place a flat plate or a same size cake pan on top of the cheese. Press to drain some more whey, pour it off, and place weights such as food cans on the plate to compress the cheese.

Refrigerate the cheese for a few hours or overnight, pouring off whey as it collects. Open the cheesecloth, put a plate over the cheese and flip the pan upside down to unmold the cheese. Remove the cheesecloth and serve.

Bread Cheese: Place under a broiler until the top is speckled with brown. Serve warm or cold.

SANDWICHES
Voileivät

A Finnish sandwich is quite different from an American sandwich. It is always open-faced and eaten with a knife and a fork. Sandwiches of this type are available everywhere from the finest restaurants to the smallest coffee shops. A nicely decorated sandwich is served as an appetizer, a couple of sandwiches on a plate make a nice lunch, sandwiches are often served as a snack at a coffee party, and even after a dinner party a snack of a sandwich is often served for the road home.

The bread used for sandwiches is a dense white or dark bread. Delicatessens often carry square, thinly sliced German or Danish type breads, which are ideal, but any kind of dense bread is suitable. If the crust is hard, it is removed. The bread is cut very thinly and usually buttered very lightly with soft butter, but you can substitute a thin layer of mayonnaise. Very often, the bread is covered with a leaf of soft Boston lettuce or green leaf lettuce. After that, your preference and imagination can take over. Ingredients are always folded or rolled appetizingly on the bread. Sandwiches are often garnished with dill sprigs or parsley sprigs and thin wedges of tomato or slices of orange for color. Here are some suggestions for popular traditional sandwich toppings.

HAM SANDWICH

Kinkkuvoileipä

Leaf of soft lettuce
Boiled or smoked ham slices
A cooked prune or half a slice of orange
Cucumber slices
Parsley sprigs

ROAST BEEF SANDWICH

Paistivoileipä

Leaf of soft lettuce
Roast beef slices
Cucumber pickles
A few gratings of fresh horseradish or half a teaspoon prepared horseradish
Parsley sprigs

EGG AND ANCHOVY SANDWICH

Muna-anjovisvoileipä

Leaf of soft lettuce
Slices of hard-boiled eggs
3-4 fillets of Scandinavian anchovies
Cucumber slices
Dill sprigs

SALMON SANDWICH

Lohivoileipä

Leaf of soft lettuce
Slices of smoked or salted salmon
Lemon wedge
Dill sprigs

VEGETABLE SALAD SANDWICH

Salaattivoileipä

Leaf of soft lettuce
Cooked vegetable salad (page 118)
Green pepper rings
Tomato wedge
Parsley sprigs

CHEESE SANDWICH

Juustovoileipä

Leaf of soft lettuce
Cheese slices
Slices of radish or green pepper
Parsley sprigs

HERRING SANDWICH

Sillvoileipä

Leaf of soft lettuce
3-4 pieces of herring, or herring salad (page 110)
Onion rings
Dill sprigs

Other popular toppings are tiny shrimp with dill sprigs and lemon slices, smoked fish with cold scrambled eggs and chives or dill, and liver paté with sautéed mushrooms and cucumber salad or cucumber pickles. In Finland there are also a wide variety of sausages and cold cuts, such as Italian-type mortadellas and salamis, that are used for sandwich toppings.

After a show or a party Finns often invite friends over for a late snack, or if dinner has been served early, the family is served a small bite before retiring. A selection of sandwiches makes a popular snack, and especially in winter a hot snack such as Jansson's Temptation, Custard Roll with Smoked Fish Filling, Meat Pie, Karelian Pastries or a hot sandwich is served. Hot sandwiches are usually made with meats or cooked fish and topped with plenty of grated cheese. They are then cooked in a hot oven until the cheese has melted, and served with some cucumber or tomato slices. A popular sandwich, the Opera Sandwich, is made with ground beef and topped with a fried egg, for which the recipe is included. If you use sliced ham instead of ground beef, the sandwich is called Chapel Sandwich, or *kappelivoileipä*, probably after a popular outdoor restaurant in Helsinki.

OPERA SANDWICH
Oopperavoileipä

1 slice white bread
4 ounces lean ground beef
1 tablespoon chopped onion
1 tablespoon heavy cream
Salt and pepper to taste
1 large egg
2 tablespoons butter

Mix the ground beef with onion, cream, salt and pepper. Spread on the bread slice. Cook in ½ tablespoon butter, beef side down, over medium heat, until beef is browned. Turn over and cook the bread side in 1 tablespoon of the butter until nicely browned. Remove to a plate. Cook the egg in the remaining butter, on one side only, so that the yolk makes a sauce for the sandwich. Place on top of the sandwich and serve.

SANDWICH CAKE
Voileipäkakku

Sandwich cake is often served for entertaining, and a slice of sandwich loaf also makes a nice appetizer. Fillings vary according to the availability and preference. Smoked fish filling, as in Custard Roll with Smoked Fish Filling (page 60), is often used instead of ham, in which case the cake may be decorated with lemon slices and shrimp.

1 loaf white sandwich bread, unsliced, and preferably one day old
1/4 cup cold chicken broth

HAM FILLING:
6 ounces cooked smoked ham, finely chopped
1/4 cup mayonnaise
2 teaspoons Dijon-type mustard
1 teaspoon prepared horseradish

CUCUMBER FILLING:
1 cup grated cucumber, squeezed dry
1 tablespoon chopped fresh dill
1 tablespoon chopped parsley
1 tablespoon chopped chives or grated onion
2 tablespoons sour cream or mayonnaise
2 teaspoons white vinegar
1 teaspoon sugar
1/4 teaspoon salt

EGG FILLING:
4 hard-boiled eggs, chopped
1/4 cup mayonnaise
2 tablespoons chopped fresh dill
1/4 teaspoon salt

FROSTING AND TOPPING:
8 ounces Neufchâtel cheese (light cream cheese) or cream cheese
1/4 cup sour cream or mayonnaise
1/2 cup mixed chopped fresh herbs (dill, parsley, chives)
Slices of ham and cucumber, tomato wedges
Sprigs of dill and parsley

In separate bowls, mix ingredients for each filling. With a sharp knife, remove all crusts from the bread. Cut the loaf horizontally into 4 slices. Place a slice on a plate, and sprinkle 1 tablespoon chicken broth over the slice. Spread egg filling evenly over the slice. Top with another slice of bread, sprinkle with chicken broth and spread evenly with ham filling. Repeat with the cucumber filling, and top with the last slice of bread. Wrap the loaf tightly with plastic wrap and put a light weight on top, such as a small cutting board weighted with a food can. Refrigerate overnight.

For the frosting, mix softened cream cheese well with sour cream and spread the top and sides of the loaf with the mixture. Sprinkle the sides with mixture of fresh herbs and press with a spatula to make them adhere. Decorate the top with rolled slices of ham, sliced cucumbers, tomato wedges and sprigs of dill and parsley. Slice as cake to serve. Serves 8.

VI.
DESSERTS

SWEETENED WHIPPED CREAM
Kermavaahto

1 cup chilled heavy cream
2 tablespoons powdered sugar
1 teaspoon vanilla

Whip the cream, sugar and vanilla until the mixture thickens lightly, but be careful not to whip it so much that it becomes stiff. Serve with desserts.

RHUBARB PUDDING
Raparperikiisseli

3 cups rhubarb, peeled and cut into ½-inch slices
3 cups water
¾ cup sugar
3 tablespoons potato starch or cornstarch
⅓ cup cold water

Place the rhubarb, 3 cups water and sugar into a stainless steel or enameled saucepan, bring to boil, lower the heat, cover, and let simmer until the rhubarb is soft, about 30 minutes. In a small bowl mix the starch with the cold water and gradually whisk it into the rhubarb mixture. Bring back to boil and cook until mixture thickens. Sprinkle with sugar to prevent skin from forming, let cool and serve with whipped cream, if desired.

CRANBERRY PUDDING
Karpalokiisseli

In Finland this pudding is made with lingonberry juice, but cranberry juice makes a tasty substitute.

3 cups cranberry juice

3 tablespoons potato starch or cornstarch
⅓ cup cold water
½ cup sugar

In a saucepan bring the cranberry juice to boil. Mix the potato starch with the water and stir into the boiling juice. Stir until liquid thickens. Remove from heat and add sugar to taste. Let cool, chill and serve with sweetened whipped cream.

APRICOT PUDDING
Aprikoosikiisseli

1 cup dried apricots
5 cups water
¾ cup sugar
3 tablespoons potato starch or cornstarch

Rinse the apricots and bring them to a boil with 5 cups water in an enameled or stainless steel saucepan. Lower the heat and simmer the apricots until they are very soft, about 30 minutes. Add the sugar and beat with a wire whisk to break up apricots into small pieces. Mix the starch with a ¼ cup of cold water and pour into the apricots, stirring constantly. Bring to bubbling boil, remove from heat, sprinkle with sugar to prevent skin from forming, and let cool. Serve with whipped cream.

MIXED FRUIT PUDDING
Sekahedelmäkiisseli

½ pound mixed dried fruit
4 cups water
1 cinnamon stick
½ cup sugar
3 tablespoons potato starch or cornstarch
⅓ cup cold water

Rinse the mixed fruit and place it in a saucepan with 4 cups water, cinnamon stick and sugar, bring to boil, lower the heat and let simmer, covered, until the fruit is tender, about 1 hour. Mix the potato starch with ⅓ cup cold water and stir it gradually into the mixed fruit. Keep stirring, until the mixture thickens and begins to boil. Remove from heat, sprinkle with sugar to prevent skin from forming, and let cool. Remove the cinnamon stick before serving. Serve with lightly whipped cream.

PRUNE PUDDING
Luumukiisseli

12-ounce package of pitted prunes
4 cups water
1 cinnamon stick
¾ cup sugar
3 tablespoons potato starch or cornstarch
⅓ cup cold water
1 tablespoon lemon juice

Cook the prunes in the water with the cinnamon stick and the sugar for 30-40 minutes or until very soft. If you want the prunes to remain whole, remove to a serving dish before proceeding with the recipe. Remove the cinnamon stick. Mix the starch with ⅓ cup cold water and whisk this into the cooking liquid. Bring to a boil, stirring, until the pudding thickens and begins to boil. Remove from heat and add the lemon juice. Pour over prunes in serving dish, sprinkle with sugar to prevent skin from forming, and cool. Serve with lightly sweetened whipped cream.

BLUEBERRY SOUP
Mustikkakeitto

In Finland this soup is made from the smaller, wild blueberries that grow in the woods. The American cultivated blueberries make a nice soup, but some lemon juice is needed to bring out the flavor. In Finland the soup is served on its own as a dessert, or over a slice of pancake, or over the smaller dessert pancakes.

1 pint blueberries, washed
3 cups water
¾ cup sugar
2 tablespoons lemon juice
2 tablespoons potato starch or cornstarch
⅓ cup cold water

In a saucepan bring the blueberries to boil with the water, lower the heat and let simmer for 10-15 minutes. Strain out the blueberries, extracting as much juice as possible, return the soup to the saucepan, add the sugar and lemon juice and bring to boil. Mix the potato starch or cornstarch with the cold water and pour the mixture into the soup while beating vigorously with a wire whisk. Bring to boil until mixture bubbles and remove from the heat. Let cool, pour into a serving dish and sprinkle with sugar.

RAISIN SOUP
Rusinakeitto

This is an old-fashioned Christmas dish, always served with rice porridge. Before refrigeration and quick transportation raisins and dried fruit were often the only fruit available in the middle of winter. Raisin soup was considered part of a festive meal and always served in celebrations like weddings. Often some rice is cooked in the soup, especially if it is to be served alone as a dessert.

1 cup seedless raisins
4 cups water
½ cup sugar
1 cinnamon stick
(1 tablespoon rice)
1½ tablespoons potato starch or cornstarch
¼ cup cold water

In a saucepan cook the raisins in the water with the sugar and the cinnamon stick until the raisins are plump and done, about 30 minutes. (If you use rice, add it after 10 minutes of cooking). Mix the potato starch with the cold water and stir into the soup. Bring back to boil and remove from heat. Sprinkle with sugar to prevent skin from forming, and let cool. Serve with rice porridge.

PRUNE WHIP
Luumukohokas

1 12-ounce package pitted dried prunes
½ cup sugar
1 tablespoon lemon juice
Pinch of salt
3 egg whites

Place the prunes in a saucepan and add water to barely cover. Bring to boil over medium heat, cover and let cook for 20 minutes, or until prunes are very soft. Drain the prunes, reserving the water. Puree the prunes in a food processor or blender, adding enough of the cooking water to process the prunes. Return the prune puree back to the saucepan, add the sugar, and heat while stirring, until the prune mixture thickens. Remove from heat, add the lemon juice and let cool.

Preheat oven to 350°F. Whip the egg whites with a pinch of salt until stiff, stir a quarter of the egg whites into the prunes and fold the prune mixture into the egg whites. Butter a 1-quart souffle dish, fill with the prune mixture and place it in another baking pan. Fill the baking pan with hot water to about an inch from the bottom. Place the pan in the oven for about 45 minutes, or until the prune whip is well puffed and browned. Serve warm with custard sauce.

CUSTARD SAUCE
Vaniljakastike

1 tablespoon cornstarch
¼ cup sugar
2 cups milk
1 large egg
1 teaspoon vanilla

In a saucepan whisk together the cornstarch, sugar, milk and egg. Place over medium heat and stir with a wooden spoon until the mixture thickens slightly. Remove from heat and stir in the vanilla. Let cool, cover with a plastic wrap and refrigerate. Serve with desserts.

POACHED PEARS WITH BUTTERSCOTCH SAUCE
Päärynät kinuskikastikeessa

4 peeled, cored, halved pears
1 cup water
½ cup sugar
Cinnamon stick

In a 10-inch skillet bring the water to boil with the sugar and the cinnamon stick. Add the pears, cover, and simmer for 20 minutes, turning pears occasionally, until they are soft. Drain pears and cool. Serve with warm butterscotch sauce.

BUTTERSCOTCH SAUCE
Kinuskikastike

¼ cup dark brown sugar
¼ cup light corn syrup or pancake syrup
¾ cup heavy cream
2 tablespoons butter
1 teaspoon vanilla

In a small saucepan cook the sugar, the syrup and the cream until the sugar is melted and the sauce thickened slightly. Remove from heat and stir in the butter and the vanilla. Serve warm over poached pears, or use cold as a cake filling.

STRAWBERRY SNOW
Mansikkalumi

1 pint fresh strawberries
½ cup water
½ teaspoon unflavored gelatine
2 egg whites
½ cup sugar
½ cup heavy cream, whipped

Soak the gelatine in ¼ cup water until soft. Heat the rest of the water and in it dissolve the gelatine. Let cool and refrigerate for 5 minutes. Meanwhile, clean and hull the strawberries, save a few for decoration and finely chop the rest either by hand or in a food processor.

Beat the egg whites until soft peaks are formed, and gradually add the sugar. Continue beating until stiff peaks are formed when the beater is lifted. Stir the gelatine mixture into the strawberries and fold the strawberries into the egg whites carefully with an under-and-over motion. Fold in the whipped cream. Serve at once decorated with fresh strawberry slices, or freeze. Stir once after 5 minutes in the freezer.

APPLE SNOW
Omenalumi

2 egg whites
¼ cup sugar
1 cup unsweeetened applesauce
Cinnamon for sprinkling

Beat the egg whites with a wire whisk or an electric mixer until soft peaks are formed. Gradually add the sugar and continue to beat until stiff peaks are formed when the beater is lifted. Fold in the applesauce with an under-and-over motion, trying not to deflate the egg whites. Serve at once, sprinkled with cinnamon. The dessert can be frozen and served as a sherbet.

DESSERT PANCAKES
Ohukaiset

In Finland these pancakes are cooked in a special cast iron pan with small round sections, called a plett pan. They are available in some specialty stores and many stores catering to Scandinavian customers. Otherwise, cook the pancakes in small omelet pans. Since the batter is very thin and there is no baking powder in it, the pancakes are very thin and fragile. The idea is to get the pancakes so thin that the edges are lacy. They are a very popular summertime dessert.

2 cups milk
1 cup flour, preferably granulated
3 large eggs
2 tablespoons sugar
½ teaspoon salt
2 tablespoons butter

Mix the batter with a wire whisk or use a blender. Beat all ingredients, except the butter, until well mixed. Set aside for 15 minutes. Melt the butter in the pancake pan and add it to the batter, beating well. Cook small pancakes in the pan, turning once, until nicely brown on both sides. It is not necessary to grease the pan in between the pancakes, since the butter is already in the batter. If you pour the batter into a pitcher, it is easier to pour a proper amount in the pan. Serve the pancakes sprinkled with sugar or with strawberry sauce. (next page)

STRAWBERRY SAUCE
Mansikkakastike

1 pint strawberries
¾ cup sugar

Rinse and drain the berries well. Hull the berries and if they are large, halve or quarter them. In a stainless steel saucepan layer the berries with the sugar and let stand for an hour or two, or until the berries have released some of their juices. On very low heat bring to boil and let simmer for 15 minutes. Do not stir. Let cool and serve with pancakes.

OVEN PANCAKE
Pannukakku

2 tablespoons butter
4 cups milk
4 large eggs
4 tablespoons sugar
1 teaspoon salt
¾ cup flour

Preheat oven to 400°F. Put the butter in a 9x12" baking pan and set the pan in the oven until butter is melted. Take the pan out of the oven and swirl the butter around to coat the pan. In a bowl beat the eggs and add the milk, sugar, and salt. Whisk in the flour. Pour the mixture into the baking pan and bake for 40 minutes, or until nicely puffed and browned on top. Pancake will sink as it cools and is very custardy in texture. Serve cut in squares, with strawberry sauce or cinnamon sugar. In Finland this pancake is often served with blueberry soup.

ALAND PANCAKE
Ahvenanmaan pannukakku

Aland is a large group of islands in the Baltic Sea between Finland and Sweden. It belongs to Finland, but is largely autonomous and Swedish is the spoken language.

4 cups milk
⅓ cup quick-cooking farina
3 large eggs
¼ cup sugar
½ teaspoon salt
1 cup flour
1 teaspoon ground cardamom
1 teaspoon vanilla

In a saucepan heat 2 cups of the milk and stir in the farina. Let cook, stirring, until thickens. Sprinkle with sugar and let cool.

Preheat oven to 400°F. Beat the eggs and the sugar until foamy, add the farina, the flour, and the rest of the ingredients. Pour into a buttered 9"x 12" baking pan and bake for about 30 minutes, or until puffed and lightly browned. Best when served warm with a dessert soup, such as blueberry soup or raisin soup, or serve the pancake sprinkled with sugar.

FRENCH TOAST
Köyhät ritarit

French toast, or poor knights, as they are called in Finland, is a common dessert in Finland, served with whipped cream and jam, or sprinkled with sugar and cinnamon. It is made with a white French type loaf, called ranskanleipä in Finland (page 154), but any dense white loaf is acceptable. Finnish cardamom braid, pulla, is also very good for this dish.

1 large egg
1½ cups milk
6 slices white bread
3 tablespoons butter

TOPPING:
Lightly whipped sweetened cream
Strawberry or raspberry jam
***or* 2 tablespoons sugar**
½ teaspoon cinnamon

Whisk the egg and the milk together well and soak the bread slices in it until thoroughly moistened. Melt the butter in a large skillet and sauté the bread slices until they are golden brown on both sides. Top as desired and serve immediately.

CREAMY RICE PORRIDGE
Riisipuuro

This dish is a must at a Finnish Christmas table. It is served as a dessert, and one peeled almond is always mixed in the porridge. Whoever finds the almond will get married the following year, or otherwise be followed with good luck.

½ cup rice
1 cup water
3 cups milk
1 cinnamon stick
¾ teaspoon salt
(1 teaspoon vanilla)
(¼ cup heavy cream)
1 peeled almond

In a double boiler over simmering water cook the rice in water, covered, until the water has been absorbed, about 15 minutes. Add milk, cinnamon stick and salt, cover and let cook for 2 hours, stirring occasionally. Porridge will be very creamy, and the rice grains broken down. For festive occasions add the vanilla and some heavy cream, and for Christmas, add one peeled almond. Serve sprinkled with sugar and cinnamon, with whipped cream, or with a dessert soup such as blueberry soup or raisin soup.

CRANBERRY-RYE PUDDING
Ruismarjapuuro

4 cups bottled cranberry juice
¼ cup sugar
½ teaspoon salt
1 cup rye flour
2 tablespoons dark corn syrup or pancake syrup

In a double boiler mix cranberry juice with the sugar and the salt, whisk in the rye flour and bring to boil over hot water, stirring often, until it thickens. Cover and let cook for one hour over low heat, stirring occasionally. Sweeten with the syrup and let cool. Serve sprinkled with sugar and with half-and-half or whipped cream.

WHIPPED BERRY PUDDING
Vatkattu marjapuuro, Vispipuuro

3 cups bottled cranberry juice
¼ cup sugar
½ cup uncooked farina
⅛ teaspoon salt

In a 2-quart saucepan bring the cranberry juice to boil. Add sugar and salt and sprinkle in the farina, whisking with a wire whip. Reduce heat and simmer for 10 minutes, stirring, until the mixture thickens. Transfer the mixture into the bowl of an electric mixer and beat at high speed for 10-15 minutes, until the pudding is very fluffy and light pink in color. Pour into serving dishes and serve at room temperature with half-and-half or whipped cream, and sprinkled with sugar.

WHIPPED APRICOT PUDDING
Vatkattu aprikoosipuuro

1 cup dried apricots
3 cups water
½ cup sugar
¼ teaspoon salt
½ cup farina

In a saucepan, simmer the rinsed apricots in the water about 30 minutes, or until the apricots are very soft. Add the sugar and salt and whisk in the farina. Let cook for about 10 minutes, stirring often. Let cool. Beat the pudding with an electric mixer until light and fluffy. Serve with milk or cream and sprinkled with sugar.

VICTORIA PUDDING
Viktoriakiisseli

In poor times in Finland rice was a prized grain, and a lot of desserts and festive dishes made use of this specialty.

¼ cup rice
½ cup water
1½ cups milk
1 teaspoon unflavored gelatine
2 tablespoons cold water
¼ cup sugar
1 teaspoon vanilla
½ cup heavy cream, whipped

On top of a double boiler over simmering water cook the rice in the water under cover until the water is absorbed, about 15 minutes. Stir in the milk and let cook over low heat, stirring often, until the milk is absorbed and the rice is very soft. Soak the gelatine in the cold water until thickened and stir it well into the hot rice. Stir in the sugar and vanilla and let cool. Fold in the whipped cream and spoon the dessert into individual dishes. Refrigerate until firm. Unmold the desserts onto serving plates and spoon over fresh strawberry sauce or chocolate sauce (pages 142 and 147).

COURT DESSERT
Hovijälkiruoka

3-4 small meringues (on page 204) per person
Sweetened whipped cream
Chocolate sauce

In individual dessert dishes layer the meringues with the sweetened whipped cream. Pour about one tablespoon of chocolate sauce over the meringues. Serve immediately.

CHOCOLATE SAUCE
Suklaakastike

¼ cup cocoa
½ cup sugar
¼ cup heavy cream
¼ cup water
1 teaspoon cornstarch
½ teaspoon vanilla

Mix all the ingredients except vanilla together in a small saucepan. Bring to boil stirring, and cook until the mixture thickens and becomes shiny. Stir in the vanilla. Serve warm or cold. Makes about 1 cup.

PARSON'S MAKESHIFT DESSERT
Pappilan hätävara

I had to include this dessert, as it has such a lovely name, and is quite popular besides. When the parsonage was the pillar of society and the service always had to be above reproach, this recipe came in handy in a pinch, when dessert was needed.

Vanilla wafers, or other cookies or rusks
About 1 cup fruit juice or milk
1 cup heavy cream, whipped and flavored with 1 teaspoon vanilla
⅓ -½ cup strawberry or raspberry jam or jelly

On a plate soak the cookies, one layer at a time, in the fruit juice or milk, until they are half softened, and transfer them into a serving bowl. Spread whipped cream and some jam between each layer, finishing with the whipped cream. Decorate with some of the jam or fruit, cover and refrigerate for an hour before serving.

CHARLOTTE RUSSE
Charlotte Russe

Jelly roll (on page 195)
¼ cup cold water
1 envelope unsweetened gelatine
½ cup hot milk
¼ cup sugar
2 teaspoons vanilla
1 cup heavy cream, whipped

Lightly oil a 1-quart bowl and line it with slices of jelly roll.

Soften the gelatine in cold water and stir into the hot milk until melted. Stir in the sugar and the vanilla, and when cooled, stir in the whipped cream. Pour into the bowl over the jelly roll and refrigerate until firm. Put a serving plate upside down over the dessert and invert the bowl to unmold.

EASTER PASHA
Pasha

2 egg yolks
1/3 cup heavy cream
3/4 cup sugar
4 tablespoons sweet butter
1/2 pound cream cheese or Neufchâtel cheese, softened
1/2 pound farmer cheese or pot cheese, softened
1 cup sour cream
1/2 teaspoon vanilla
1/4 cup currants or raisins
1/4 cup slivered almonds

In a saucepan whisk together the egg yolks, the heavy cream and 1/4 cup of the sugar. Place the saucepan over low heat and keep stirring until the mixture starts to thicken. Remove from heat immediately and add the cold butter by the tablespoons. You may have to return the pan over heat occasionally to help absorb the butter, but be careful not to scramble the eggs. When all the butter has been absorbed, remove from heat and let cool.

In a bowl stir together the cheeses, sour cream and 1/2 cup sugar. Add the egg mixture, vanilla, currants and almonds. Mix well.

Dampen a cheesecloth and set it over a pasha mold or a clean new clay flower pot with a drainage hole, or just a strainer, and spoon the mixture into the mold. Bring the ends of the cheesecloth up over the mixture and place a plate with a 1-pound can of food over the plate to weigh the cheese down. Place the mold on a rack over a larger plate, and refrigerate until the next day.

Unmold and remove the cheesecloth to serve. Pasha is traditionally served with slices of sweet Easter bread.

MALTED RYE PUDDING
Mämmi

This old-fashioned dessert is traditionally served only at Easter.

6 cups water
4 cups rye flour (whole rye flour)
3 cups malted barley (available in health or natural food stores)
1 tablespoon grated orange peel
⅓ cup dark corn syrup or pancake syrup
½ teaspoon salt
¼ cup sugar
½ cup boiling water

In a 4-quart saucepan heat 2 cups of water. Whisk in 1 cup of rye flour and 1 cup malted barley. Cover and place in a warming oven at the lowest setting available (120°-140°F) for one hour.

Bring the remaining 4 cups of water to boil and stir into the mixture. Stir in the remaining 3 cups of flour and the rest of the malted barley. Cover and return to the warming oven for another hour.

Stir in the grated orange peel, the syrup and the salt, and if necessary, some more rye flour. The mixture should be the consistency of creamy porridge. Bring to boil stirring constantly to prevent scorching, and cook, stirring, for 10 minutes. Remove from heat and let cool, stirring often.

Preheat oven to 300°F. Pour the mixture into small buttered baking pans, filling each only ⅔ full. Stir ¼ cup of sugar into ½ cup of boiling water, and spoon this liquid over the mixture in the baking pans, to prevent a heavy skin from forming. Bake for 2½-3 hours. Let cool and serve at room temperature with sugar and cream. *Mämmi* is best a few days old. Serves 10-12.

VII.

BREADS AND SWEET YEAST BREADS

WHITE LOAF
Ranskanleipä

This very popular white loaf is called French bread in Finland.

1 cup warm water (110°F)
1 envelope dry yeast
1 teaspoon salt
1 teaspoon sugar
3 tablespoons butter, softened
2-2¼ cups flour

This dough is easy to make in a food processor, but of course you can also make it by hand. Dissolve the yeast in the warm water. Stir in the salt, sugar and softened butter. Beat in the flour and knead until the dough is smooth and elastic. Cover with a kitchen towel and let rise until double in bulk, about 1½-2 hours. Punch down, and on a floured board knead and shape it into a round loaf about 9 inches in diameter. Cover it with a kitchen towel and let rise for about 45 minutes.

Preheat oven to 400°F. Pat the loaf down with hands and using hands or a rolling pin stretch it into round flat sheet about ½ inch thick. Starting from one side roll it into a loaf. Place it seam side down on a baking sheet covered with parchment paper, or lightly greased, and with a sharp knife cut a ½-inch deep slash from one end of the loaf to the other. Place immediately in oven, and bake until nicely browned and the loaf sounds hollow when tapped with a finger, about 25 minutes. Cool without cover to get a crisp crust.

ROUND WHEAT LOAVES
Nisukakko

When wheat was scarce and most bread was baked from rye flour, wheat loaf was a special treat, baked for festive occasions. This anise-flavored bread is good enough to replace sweet rolls when buttered and served with coffee or tea. In some areas of Finland it is called vinttikakko.

2 cups milk
2 tablespoons butter
2 teaspoons salt
1 teaspoon ground anise seed
2 envelopes dry yeast
¼ cup warm water (110°F)
4½-5 cups flour

Scald the milk until small bubbles form on the side of the saucepan, pour into a mixing bowl, add the salt, butter, and anise seed, and let cool until lukewarm. In a small bowl dissolve the yeast in the warm water and add to the milk. Add half the flour and beat with an electric mixer until smooth. Stir in the rest of the flour and beat with a wooden spoon until the dough forms a ball. Turn the dough onto a floured board and knead until smooth and elastic. Put the dough back into the mixing bowl and let rise in a warm place, covered with a kitchen towel, for 1½-2 hours or until double in bulk.

Turn the dough onto a floured board and knead until smooth. Divide it in two, and roll each part into a round loaf. Pat them down with your hands and prick them all over with a fork. Transfer the loaves onto a baking sheet covered with parchment paper or lightly greased, sprinkle them with flour and cover with a kitchen towel. Let rise for 45 minutes.

Preheat oven to 375°F. Bake the loaves for 20-25 minutes, or until lightly browned and a loaf sounds hollow when tapped with a finger. Cool on a rack, covered with a kitchen towel.

POPPY SEED ROLLS
Vehnäsämpylät

1 envelope dry yeast
¼ cup warm water (110°F)

½ cup milk
2 tablespoons sugar
½ teaspoon salt
1 large egg, lightly beaten
2-2½ cups flour
6 tablespoons butter, softened

FILLING AND GLAZE:
2 tablespoons butter
2 tablespoons heavy cream
2 teaspoons poppy seeds

Dissolve the yeast in the warm water. Heat the milk to lukewarm and in a bowl mix the milk with the sugar, salt and the beaten egg. Stir in the flour and knead the dough until it forms a ball. Add the softened butter in bits, and knead until the butter has been absorbed and the dough is smooth and elastic. Cover and let stand for 20 minutes.

On a floured board roll the dough into a rectangle about ½ inch thick and 10" x 20" in size. Melt 2 tablespoons of butter with the heavy cream and brush all over the dough. Fold the dough twice lengthwise and leave the seam underneath. Cut the dough into 2-inch pieces and place them on a baking sheet covered with parchment paper or lightly greased. Cover with a kitchen towel and let rise in a warm place for about 1 hour.

Preheat oven to 375°F. Brush the rolls with the remainder of the filling mixture and sprinkle on the poppy seeds. Bake for about 10-15 minutes, or until nicely browned. Cool on a rack covered with a kitchen towel.

BREAKFAST BUNS
Aamiaissämpylät

2 cups milk
½ cup cracked wheat or toasted wheat breakfast cereal
2 teaspoons salt

1 tablespoon crushed caraway seeds
2 envelopes dry yeast
¼ cup warm water (110°F)
1¾ cups bread flour or all-purpose flour
2 cups whole wheat flour
¼ cup vegetable oil

Heat the milk until small bubbles form at the side of the pan. Pour into a bowl and add the breakfast cereal, salt and caraway seeds. Cool until lukewarm. Dissolve the yeast in warm water and add to the milk. Add the bread flour and beat with an electric mixer until smooth. Add the whole wheat flour and the oil and mix with a wooden spoon until the dough forms a ball. Turn onto a floured board and knead until smooth. Return into the bowl, cover with a kitchen towel and let rise in a warm place until double in bulk, about 1½ hours.

Turn the dough onto a board, knead and divide it in two. Roll each part into a thick strand, and cut each strand into 6 small pieces. Shape the pieces into small buns. Place the buns on baking sheets lined with parchment paper or lightly greased. Cover with kitchen towels and let rise until double in bulk, about 45 minutes.

Preheat oven to 425°F. Bake the buns for about 10 minutes, or until lightly browned, and cool on a rack covered with kitchen towels.

LIGHT RYE BREAD
Hiivaleipä

If you have a food processor, this bread is very easy to prepare, and only takes about 1½ to 2 hours from start to finish. This way, you can have a fresh loaf of bread for dinner, even if pressed for time. Of course you can also make the dough by hand. This is a recipe for one loaf, easily done in a food processor, but the recipe can be easily doubled and made by hand or with a food mixer.

1 cup warm water (110°F)
1 envelope dry yeast
1 teaspoon salt
1 teaspoon sugar
1 tablespoon vegetable oil
1 cup rye flour
1½-2 cups all-purpose flour

In a food processor dissolve the yeast in the warm water, add the salt, the sugar, and the oil and pulsate once. Add the rye flour and 1½ cups of the all-purpose flour and process until dough forms a ball. If the machine begins to stall, add a little more flour. Place the dough in an oiled mixing bowl and let rise in a warm place, loosely covered with plastic wrap, for 30 minutes. On a floured board knead the dough and shape it into a round loaf. Place on a baking sheet covered with parchment paper or lightly greased, prick all over with a fork, sprinkle with flour, cover with a kitchen towel and let rise in warm place for 30 minutes.

Preheat oven to 375°F. Bake the bread for 30 minutes, or until it sounds hollow when tapped with a finger. Cool on a wire rack, covered with kitchen towel.

Variation: The variations on this bread are almost endless. You can substitute the rye flour with whole wheat flour, barley flour, or any combination of flours you have at hand. You can substitute half of the whole wheat flour with cracked wheat cereal or oatmeal. You can add 1 teaspoon caraway seeds or anise seeds, or both, for flavor. You can add a couple of tablespoons of bran, if you want more bran in your bread. You can also substitute the water with milk.

WHOLE WHEAT LOAF
Grahamleipä

2 cups warm water (110°F)
2 envelopes dry yeast
2 teaspoons salt
2 teaspoons caraway seeds
1 tablespoon dark corn syrup or pancake syrup
1 tablespoon vegetable oil
⅔ cup wheat bran
1 1/3 cup flour
2-2½ cups whole wheat flour or rye flour

In a mixing bowl dissolve the yeast in the warm water. Add the rest of the ingredients and knead the dough on a floured board until it is smooth and elastic. The dough will be sticky. Place it back into the bowl, cover it with a plastic wrap and let rise for 1½ to 2 hours, or until double in bulk. Knead the dough on a floured board until it is smooth, and shape it into a loaf. Place it into a buttered 2-quart loaf pan, sprinkle it with wheat bran and cover it with a kitchen towel. Let rise again about 1 hour.

Preheat oven to 375°F. Bake the loaf for about 45-60 minutes, or until nicely browned. Cool the bread 15 minutes before unmolding on a rack to cool. Cover it with a kitchen towel.

MIXED GRAIN LOAVES
Sekahiivaleipä

2 cups warm water (110°F)
2 envelopes dry yeast
2 teaspoons salt
2 tablespoons vegetable oil or melted butter
1 cup oatmeal
2 cups bread flour or all purpose flour
1 cup whole wheat flour
1 cup rye flour

In a mixing bowl dissolve the yeast in the warm water. Add the salt, oil, oatmeal and half of the bread flour and beat with an electric mixer until smooth. Add the rest of the flours and stir with a wooden spoon until the dough forms a ball. Turn onto a floured board and knead until the dough is smooth. It will remain somewhat sticky. Put the dough back into the mixing bowl, cover with a kitchen towel and let rise in a warm place for 1½-2 hours, or until double in bulk.

Turn onto a floured board, knead until smooth and form into two round loaves. Transfer them to a baking sheet covered with parchment paper or lightly greased. Prick them all over with a fork, sprinkle them with flour and cover with a kitchen towel. Let them rise in a warm place for about 45 minutes. Preheat oven to 375°F. Bake the loaves for 30 minutes or until lightly browned and loaves sound hollow when tapped with a finger. Cool on a rack covered with a kitchen towel.

POTATO RYE BREAD
Perunalimppu

3 medium potatoes, peeled and cut into chunks
Water
2 envelopes dry yeast
¼ cup warm potato cooking water (110°F)
½ cup barley malt (available in health or natural food stores)
¼ cup dark corn syrup or pancake syrup
2 teaspoons salt
1 teaspoon caraway seeds
1 cup buttermilk
3 cups all-purpose flour
3 cups rye flour

In a small saucepan cook the potatoes with water to cover until they are tender, when tested with a fork. Drain, but save the cooking water. Turn them into a large bowl. With a potato masher or a fork mash the potatoes, and add enough cooking water to create the consistency of regular mashed potatoes. Let cool to lukewarm. In ¼ cup of the potato water dissolve the yeast and add to the potatoes. Mix in the rest of the ingredients. Add enough rye flour to get a fairly stiff dough. Knead on a floured board until smooth. Return dough to the bowl, sprinkle it with flour, cover with a kitchen towel, and let rise in a warm place until double in bulk, about 2 hours.

Turn the dough onto a floured board, knead, and shape into 2 round loaves. Cover a baking sheet with parchment paper, or grease it lightly, and place the loaves on the baking sheet. Sprinkle them with flour, prick them all over with a fork, cover with a kitchen towel, and let rise for one hour.

Preheat oven to 350°F. Bake the loaves for about 40-45 minutes, or until they sound hollow when tapped with a finger. Cool on a wire rack covered with a kitchen towel.

SOUR RYE BREAD
Hapanleipä

You could almost say that sour rye bread is the Finnish national bread. It dates back hundreds of years, when yeast was not available and the sour starter was kept from one baking to the next. Rye is a grain that along with oats survives the long cold winters over most of Finland. After the grain was harvested and milled, the bread was baked in big batches, a hundred loaves at a time, and stored strung through poles that were hung from the ceiling. That is why the bread has a hole in the middle. The bread was baked quite thin, so that it dried quickly and kept well. The Finnish sour rye has a taste that cannot easily be duplicated, unless you are willing to spend years perfecting your starter. Here is a version that uses Finnish sour rye crackers for starter, and when the longing for a sour rye bread strikes, it tastes quite good.

10 dark Finn Crisp crackers (available in many supermarkets and stores catering to Scandinavian customers), ground into crumbs in a food processor or blender, about ½ cup
1 3/4 cups warm water
3½-4 cups whole rye flour (rye meal)
2 envelopes dry yeast
¼ cup warm water (110°F)
2 teaspoons salt

Mix the cracker crumbs with 1¾ cups warm water in a bowl, stir in ½ cup rye flour, cover with plastic wrap and let stay in room temperature for 48 hours. The mixture will start to bubble. After 24 hours stir the mixture and add ¼ cup of rye flour to feed the starter. After 12 hours or so, add another ¼ cup of rye flour. At this point you may refrigerate the dough for 1-2 days. Bring it to room temperature before continuing.

Two hours before finishing the dough add another ¼ cup rye flour to refresh the starter. Dissolve the yeast in the warm water and add it to the mixture along with salt and enough rye flour to make a soft dough. Knead the dough well, but do not add too much flour, as the dough should be very soft. It will stick to your hands. On a floured board form the dough into 2 round loaves. Line a baking sheet with parchment paper, sprinkle it with rye flour, transfer one loaf on the baking sheet, sprinkle it with flour and with a rolling pin roll it to a round loaf about 3/4-inch thick. With a biscuit cutter or a glass cut a hole in the middle. Prick the loaf all over with a toothpick and cover it with a kitchen towel. Do the same with the other round. Let the loaves rise in a warm place until they are about one inch thick, 2-3 hours. They will not rise any more in the oven.

Preheat oven to 350°F. Bake the loaves for 30-35 minutes. Cool on a rack covered with a kitchen towel.

Save the pieces of dough in the middle and use them for the next batch of bread as a starter. Wrap them in plastic and refrigerate, if you plan to use them in a couple of days. Otherwise, freeze them, and next time baking defrost them in 1 cup of warm water. You use this starter instead of the crackers.

CHRISTMAS RYE BREAD (Buttermilk Rye Bread)
Joululimppu (Piimälimppu)

2 envelopes dry yeast
¼ cup warm water (110°F)
4 cups buttermilk
1 cup dark corn syrup or pancake syrup
1½ tablespoons salt
1 tablespoon caraway seeds
1 tablespoon fennel seeds
2 tablespoons grated orange peel
5 cups all-purpose flour or bread flour
4-4½ cups rye flour

Dissolve the yeast in the warm water and add into the buttermilk in a large mixing bowl, along with the syrup and the spices. Add half of the all-purpose flour and beat well with an electric mixer. Add the rye flour and the rest of the all purpose flour, and stir with a wooden spoon until the dough forms a ball. Turn onto a floured board and knead until the dough is smooth. Add flour as necessary, but rye dough will always be tacky, so do not expect the dough to come clear off the hands. The dough should be fairly stiff. Return dough to the mixing bowl, sprinkle some flour on the top and cover it with a kitchen towel. Let rise in a warm place until double in bulk, about 2-3 hours.

Turn the dough onto a floured board and knead until smooth. Divide the dough into two or four pieces and roll the pieces into round loaves. This dough makes either two large or four smaller round loaves. Place the loaves on one or two baking sheets lined with parchment paper or greased lightly. Sprinkle the loaves with flour and cover them with kitchen towels. Let rise in a warm place until double in bulk, about one hour.

Preheat oven to 350°F. Bake about one hour for the large loaves, 45 minutes for the smaller ones, or until loaves sound hollow when tapped. Sometimes the loaves are brushed midway through the baking with a mixture of syrup and hot water, and again after the bread is done. Cool on a rack covered with kitchen towel, or with foil, if the breads are tacky with syrup.

FLATBREAD
Rieska

Flatbreads are quick breads that are made without yeast. They are especially popular in northern and eastern Finland, where there are practically as many varieties of these breads as there are cooks. They are often made with barley flour, but rye or whole wheat flour can be used as well.

2 cups barley flour or combine 1 cup rye flour and 1 cup all-purpose flour
1 teaspoon salt
2 teaspoons baking powder
1 cup light cream or milk
2 tablespoons melted butter or oil

Preheat oven to 450°F. In a bowl mix the flour with the salt and baking powder. Add the cream and butter and mix until you get a soft dough. Line a baking sheet with parchment paper, or grease it lightly, dust it with flour, and with floured hands pat the dough into a big circle about ½ inch thick. Prick all over with fork and bake for about 10 minutes, or until lightly browned. Serve hot with butter.

POTATO FLATBREAD
Perunarieska

1 cup mashed potatoes
½ teaspoon salt
1 large egg
1-1¼ cup barley flour or whole wheat flour or combine ½ cup all-purpose flour with ½ cup rye flour

Preheat oven to 450°F. If the mashed potatoes are very stiff, stir in some milk to make a fairly creamy mixture. Beat in the salt and egg and enough of the flour to make a smooth dough. Line a baking sheet with parchment paper, or grease it lightly, and sprinkle it with flour. With floured hands pat the dough into one big circle about ½ inch thick. Prick all over with a fork and bake for 10-15 minutes, or until lightly browned. Serve hot with butter.

WATER RINGS
Vesirinkelit

2 cups warm water (110°F)
2 envelopes dry yeast
2 teaspoons salt
1 tablespoon caraway seeds or ½ tablespoon crushed fennel seeds
3½-4 cups flour

In a mixing bowl dissolve the yeast in the warm water. Add the salt and the caraway seeds and beat in half the flour. Gradually add the rest of the flour, stirring with a wooden spoon, until the dough forms a ball. Turn the dough onto a floured board and knead until smooth and elastic, adding some flour if necessary. Return the dough to the mixing bowl, cover with a kitchen towel and let rise in a warm place until double in bulk, 1 to 1½ hours.

Turn the dough onto a floured board, knead and roll the dough into long strands the thickness of a finger. Cut the strands to about 10-inch pieces and shape a ring out of every piece, pressing the ends together well. Let rise under a kitchen towel for about 45 minutes.

Preheat oven to 400°F. Heat 4-6 cups water in a deep skillet, add 1-2 teaspoons salt, and lower a few rings at a time into the boiling water. Cook about 1 minute, turning them over once. When they are puffed up, take them out with a slotted spoon and place them on a baking sheet lined with parchment paper. Bake for 20 minutes or until light brown.

CARDAMOM COFFEE BRAID
Pulla

This Finnish staple, also called vehnäpitko, is served whenever coffee is served, and in many families still baked weekly at home. For festive occasions, one cup of raisins is sometimes added to the dough. In coffee parties, this bread is always served first, dry cakes and cookies are next, and last, a filled and frosted dessert cake.

1¾ cups milk
½ cup butter (1 stick), sliced
1 cup sugar
½ teaspoon salt
1 teaspoon ground cardamom
2 envelopes dry yeast
¼ cup warm water (110°F)
1 large egg
6-6½ cups flour

FOR GLAZE:
1 egg yolk
2 tablespoons milk
Sugar for sprinkling

Heat the milk in a saucepan until small bubbles form on the side of the pan. Pour the milk into a mixing bowl, add the butter, sugar, salt, and cardamom, and let cool to lukewarm. In a small bowl dissolve the yeast in warm water and add to the lukewarm milk. Lightly beat the egg and add to the milk. Add 3 cups of flour and beat with an electric mixer until smooth, about 3-4 minutes. Add 3 more cups of flour and mix with a wooden spoon until the dough forms a ball. Turn the dough onto a floured board and knead it until it is smooth and elastic, adding a little bit more flour if the dough stays too sticky. Try to manage with as little flour as possible, since too much flour makes for a stiff dough and dry bread. When the dough is smooth, return it to the bowl, cover with kitchen towel or loosely with plastic wrap, and let rise in a warm place for 1½-2 hours, or until double in bulk.

On a floured board knead the dough again until it is smooth. Divide it into 2 equal parts. Take each part and shape 3 or 4 long strands out of each part, depending on the kind of braiding you use. Braid the strands loosely, starting from the middle and working towards either end. Do not stretch. Pinch the ends together well and tuck under. Place the 2 braids on a large (12"x16") baking sheet lined with parchment paper or greased well, or use two smaller ones (10"x15"), one for each braid. Cover with a kitchen towel and let rise again for 45 minutes to an hour.

Preheat oven to 375°F. Mix the egg yolk with the milk and brush the loaves well on all sides. Sprinkle sugar along the top and bake the loaves for 25 minutes, or until nicely browned and the loaves sound hollow, when tapped on the bottom with a finger. Cool on a rack, covered with a kitchen towel.

BOSTON CAKE
Bostonkakku

This yeast cake is commonly known as Boston cake in Finland, although it is surely not known in Boston, Massachusetts. Never-

theless, it is a popular cake and no matter where the name comes from, quite delicious.

¾ cup milk
½ cup sugar
¼ teaspoon salt
½ teaspoon ground cardamom
8 tablespoons butter or margarine, softened
1 envelope dry yeast
¼ cup warm water (110°F)
1 large egg
3-3½ cups flour

FILLING:
2 tablespoons butter, melted
½ cup powdered sugar
1 teaspoon ground cinnamon

GLAZE:
1 egg yolk
2 tablespoons milk

ICING:
½ cup powdered sugar
2 teaspoons water

Heat the milk until small bubbles form on the side of the pan, pour into a mixing bowl and add the sugar, salt, cardamom and 2 tablespoons of the butter. Let cool until lukewarm. In a small bowl dissolve the yeast in the warm water and add to the milk along with the beaten egg, mix well and add the flour gradually until you get a sticky dough. Turn dough onto a board and knead until it is smooth and elastic, adding a little more flour if necessary. Add the rest of the softened butter in pieces and knead until the butter has been absorbed. You can do all this in a food processor, making sure to add more flour if the machine begins to stall. Place in a greased bowl, cover with a kitchen towel and let rise in a warm place for 1½ to 2 hours, or until double in bulk.

Turn the dough into a floured board, knead it lightly and cut it in two pieces. Roll each piece with a rolling pin to a rectangle approximately ½ inch thick and 9x12 inches in size, spread each with half the filling and roll up lengthwise. Cut each piece to slices about 2 inches thick. Butter a 9-inch cake pan and line the bottom with parchment paper. Stand the pieces on end in the cake pan, leaving about ½ inch between slices to have room for expansion. Let rise, covered loosely with a plastic wrap, for 45 minutes to an hour.

Preheat oven to 375°F. For glaze, mix the egg yolk with milk and brush the cake with the mixture before baking it in lower level of the oven for about 30 minutes, or until nicely browned.

To make filling: Beat the melted butter with powdered sugar and cinnamon until it reaches spreading consistency.

To make icing: Mix the powdered sugar with about 2 teaspoons of water, or until it reaches spreading consistency. Pour it into a plastic bag, snip a corner with scissors and drizzle the icing over the cake.

QUICK DANISH PASTRY
Pikawienerit

In the United States, these pastries are called Danish pastries. In Finland, they are called Wienerleivät, or Viennese bread. Whatever you call them, they are delicious with coffee and very popular. The original recipe calls for puff pastry dough layered with butter, and folded and rolled several times. This is a simplified recipe that produces very good results. The same dough recipe is used for Danish Slices and Danish Ring, and you might want to try all three.

½ cup butter or margarine (1 stick)
2 cups flour
¼ cup sugar

¼ teaspoon salt
2 envelopes dry yeast
¼ cup warm water (110°F)
¼ cup cold milk
1 large egg

FILLING:
3 tablespoons butter, softened
⅔ cup powdered sugar
1 teaspoon vanilla

Blend the butter and flour together until well mixed and granular, add sugar and salt and mix well. In a small bowl dissolve the yeast in the warm water, add the cold milk and the egg, and beat well together. Add this to the flour mixture and knead lightly. If the dough is too sticky, add up to another ½ cup flour, but the dough should be soft. Knead only lightly. You can also make this dough easily in a food processor, adding a little more flour if the machine begins to stall. Process only until the dough forms a ball, do not overprocess. Cover the dough with plastic wrap and chill it in refrigerator for 20 minutes.

Cut the dough into 2 equal pieces. Roll one piece with a rolling pin into a rectangle about ½ inch thick. Spread it with half the filling and roll it up jelly roll fashion, from the long side. Do the same with the other half. Line muffin tins with paper baking cups and slice the dough into 1-inch slices. Place the slices, cut side up, into the paper cups. Cover with plastic wrap and let rise for 1½-2 hours.

Preheat oven to 425°F. Bake the pastry in muffin tins for 10 minutes, or until nicely browned. Sprinkle with powdered sugar.

To make the filling: Beat together the softened butter, the powdered sugar and the vanilla until well mixed and spreading consistency. You can do this also in a food processor.

DANISH RING
Wienin rinkilä

½ cup butter or margarine (1 stick), softened
2 cups flour
¼ cup sugar
¼ teaspoon salt
2 envelopes dry yeast
¼ cup warm water (110°F)
¼ cup cold milk
1 large egg

FILLING:
4 ounces almond paste
1 tablespoon hot water
3 tablespoons butter, softened

Blend the butter and flour together until well mixed and granular, add the sugar and the salt and mix well. In a small bowl dissolve the yeast in the warm water, add the cold milk and the egg, and beat well together. Add this to the flour mixture and knead lightly. If the dough is too sticky, add up to another ½ cup flour, but the dough should be soft. Knead only lightly. You can also make the dough easily in a food processor, adding up to ½ cup more flour if the machine begins to stall. Process only until the dough forms a ball, do not overprocess. Cover with plastic wrap and chill in refrigerator for 20 minutes.

Divide the dough into two parts. Roll one part to a rectangle about ¼ inch thick and about 9" x 12" in size. Spread with half the filling. Roll up the dough jelly roll fashion, from the longer side. Do the same with the other half of the dough. On a baking sheet covered with parchment paper, or lightly greased, form the two rolls into a circle, pinching the ends together well. Make sure the seams are on the underside. Take a sharp knife and slice the ring towards the center into ½-inch slices, but don't cut the dough all the way into the center, leave the pieces attached about

½ inch. Bend every other slice inward to form a round cake, where the slices are alternately bent inward and outward.

Cover with plastic wrap and let rise in a cool place for 2 hours. Preheat oven to 375°F and bake for about 25-30 minutes, or until nicely browned. Cool on a rack and when cool, dust with powdered sugar. Serve in small wedges.

To make filling: Soften the almond paste with the hot water, add the softened butter and beat them together until they reach spreading consistency.

DANISH SLICES
Viipalewienerit

½ cup butter or margarine (1 stick), softened
2 cups flour
¼ cup sugar
¼ teaspoon salt
2 envelopes dry yeast
¼ cup warm water (110°F)
¼ cup cold milk
1 large egg

FILLING:
3½ ounces almond paste
1 tablespoon hot water
3 tablespoons butter, softened
Apricot jam

ICING:
½ cup powdered sugar
2 teaspoons cold water

Blend the butter and flour together until well mixed and granular, add sugar and salt and mix well. In a small bowl dissolve the yeast in the warm water, add the cold milk and the egg, and beat well together. Add this to the flour mixture and knead lightly. If the dough is too sticky, add up to another ½ cup flour, but the dough should be soft. Knead only lightly. You can also make this dough easily in a food processor, adding up to ½ cup more flour if the machine begins to stall. Process only until the dough forms a ball, do not overprocess. Cover with plastic wrap and chill in refrigerator for 20 minutes.

Divide the dough into two equal parts. Roll one part to a rectangle about ¼ inch thick and about 9" x 12" in size. Spread with half of the filling. Fold the dough in three, lengthwise, and place the pastry on a baking sheet lined with parchment paper or lightly greased. Make sure the last fold is facing down. With the side of your hand press a groove to run the length of the dough in the middle and fill this with apricot jam. Do the same with the other half of the dough. Cover with plastic wrap and let rise for 1½-2 hours.

Preheat oven to 425°F. Bake the pastries for 10-15 minutes, or until nicely browned. Let cool on a rack.

To make filling: Soften the almond paste with hot water, add the softened butter and beat them together until they reach spreading consistency.

For icing, mix the powdered sugar with about 2 teaspoons cold water until it reaches spreading consistency. Put the icing into a plastic bag, snip a corner with scissors, and drizzle the icing on the pastries. Slice the pastries diagonally into 2-inch pieces.

CINNAMON EARS
Korvapuustit

3/4 cup milk
8 tablespoons butter or margarine, softened
½ cup sugar
¼ teaspoon salt
½ teaspoon ground cardamom
1 envelope dry yeast

¼ cup warm water (110°F)
1 large egg
3-3½ cups flour

FILLING:

2 tablespoons butter, melted
½ cup powdered sugar
1 teaspoon ground cinnamon

GLAZE:

1 egg yolk
2 tablespoons milk

Heat the milk in a saucepan until small bubbles form on the side of the pan and pour it into a mixing bowl. Add 2 tablespoons of the butter, sugar, salt and cardamom. Let cool until lukewarm. In a small bowl dissolve the yeast in the warm water and add to the milk along with the lightly beaten egg, mix well and add the flour gradually, until you get a sticky dough. Turn it onto a floured board and knead until it is smooth and elastic, adding a little more flour if necessary. Add the rest of the softened butter in pieces and knead until the butter has been absorbed. You can do all this easily in a food processor, making sure that you add a little more flour if the machine begins to stall. Place the dough back into bowl and cover it with a kitchen towel. Let rise in a warm place for 1½ to 2 hours, or until double in bulk.

Mix the filling ingredients together. Turn the dough onto a floured board, knead lightly and cut into two equal pieces. Roll each piece to a rectangle about ½-inch thick, spread each with half the filling and roll up lengthwise jelly roll fashion. With a sharp knife, cut the roll into triangular pieces, changing the direction of the knife with every cut, but leaving the narrow end of the triangle about ½ inch wide. Turn the narrow ends of the triangular pieces up and with the dull edge of a knife or with index fingers of both hands press down, thus forming ears. Make both rolls into ears this way, place the ears on baking sheets lined with parchment paper or lightly greased, cover with a kitchen towel and let rise 45 minutes to an hour.

Preheat oven to 375°F. Beat the egg yolk with milk and brush the ears with the glaze. Bake for 15 minutes, or until nicely browned. Cool on a wire rack, covered with a kitchen towel.

BUTTER BUNS
Voipullat

These buns are very popular as coffee bread in coffee shops and offices. They are not overly sweet, and are perfect for people who do not like sugary pastries with their coffee.

¾ cup milk
¼ cup sugar
¼ teaspoon salt
½ teaspoon ground cardamom
10 tablespoons butter, softened
¼ cup warm water (110°F)
1 envelope dry yeast
1 large egg
3-3½ cups flour

In a saucepan heat the milk until small bubbles form on the side of the pan, pour into a mixing bowl and add the sugar, salt, cardamom and 2 tablespoons of butter. Stir until the milk has cooled to lukewarm and the butter has melted. Dissolve the yeast in the warm water and add to the milk along with the slightly beaten egg. Beat in the flour, and knead the dough until it is smooth. Add the rest of the softened butter in pieces and knead until the butter has been absorbed. Place the dough into a bowl, cover it loosely with plastic wrap and let rise in a warm place until double in bulk, about 1½-2 hours.

On a floured board knead the dough again and divide it to 16 pieces. Shape each piece into a round bun, and place the buns on a baking sheet covered with parchment paper, or lightly greased. Cover loosely with plastic wrap and let rise again in a warm place about 45 minutes.

Preheat oven to 400°F and bake the buns for 15 minutes, or until golden brown.

This dough can easily be prepared in a food processor. Knead the dough in the food processor with only 2 tablespoons of the butter until it forms a ball. If the machine begins to stall, add a little bit more flour. Place the dough into a bowl to rise. After the dough has risen, knead it lightly and cut it in four pieces. Place the pieces with 8 tablespoons of softened butter into the food processor, and run the machine until the butter has been absorbed. Then proceed with the recipe.

SHROVE TUESDAY BUNS
Laskiaispullat

The start of Lenten season in Finland is celebrated by going outdoors in the February cold to ski or to sleigh-ride, formerly by horse-drawn sleighs or, especially with children, downhill by small sleighs. In old times, before cotton became common, flax was an important crop for making linen clothing for summer. Long rides downhill predicted tall flax plants and a good flax crop the following summer. Common exhortation for sleigh-riders was: Pitkiä pellavia, or tall flax plants!

In present day Finland laskiaisajelut, or Shrove Tuesday rides are still often mentioned as a reason for spending the day outdoors. After the cold sleigh-ride, hot pea soup and these buns are served with hot milk—and the summer's flax crop is secure.

¾ cup milk
½ cup sugar
1 teaspoon ground cardamom
¼ teaspoon salt
4 tablespoons butter or margarine
1 envelope dry yeast

¼ cup warm water (110°F)
1 large egg
3-3½ cups flour

GLAZE:

1 egg yolk
2 tablespoons milk
Sugar for sprinkling

FILLING:

½ cup heavy cream, whipped
7 ounces almond paste or marzipan

Heat the milk until small bubbles form on the side of the pan. Pour into a bowl along with the sugar, salt, cardamom and butter. Let cool until lukewarm. In a small bowl dissolve the yeast in warm water, and add to the milk, along with the egg. With an electric mixer beat in half the flour and keep beating until the batter is smooth. Add the rest of the flour and mix with a wooden spoon until the dough forms a ball. Turn the dough onto a board and knead until smooth and elastic. Return the dough into the bowl, cover with a kitchen towel and let rise for 1½-2 hours, or until double in bulk.

On a lightly floured surface knead the dough and divide into 12 pieces. Shape the pieces into round buns. Place the buns on a baking sheet lined with parchment paper, or lightly greased. Cover with a kitchen towel and let rise again in a warm place for 45 minutes.

Preheat oven to 400°F. Mix the egg yolk with the milk and brush the buns with the glaze, sprinkle with sugar and bake for 15 minutes, or until nicely browned. Cool on a rack covered with a kitchen towel. When cool, split horizontally in half and fill with a slice of almond paste and a tablespoon of whipped cream.

CHEESE TARTS (Lingonberry Tarts)
Rahkapiirakat (Puolukkapiirakat)

You can make lingonberry tarts by filling the tarts with sweetened lingonberries instead of the cheese mixture.

PASTRY:
½ cup milk
3 tablespoons warm water
1 envelope dry yeast
2 tablespoons sugar
¼ teaspoon salt
1 large egg
2-2½ cups flour
6 tablespoons butter or margarine, softened

FILLING:
2 cups ricotta cheese (15-ounce container)
2 tablespoons heavy cream
¼ cup sugar
1 large egg
1 teaspoon vanilla
⅓ cup raisins

GLAZE:
1 egg yolk
2 tablespoons milk

Heat the milk in a saucepan until small bubbles form on the side of the pan. Let cool to lukewarm. Dissolve the yeast in the warm water and add to the milk along with the sugar, salt and egg. Mix well. Add half the flour and beat well with a wooden spoon. Add the rest of the flour and knead well. Add the softened butter in small pieces and knead until it has incorporated into the dough. You can do all this easily in a food processor, adding a little bit of flour if the machine begins to stall. Place the dough into a bowl, cover and let rise in a warm place until double in bulk, about 1½-2 hours. Knead the dough again on a lightly floured board, and divide it into 12 pieces. Roll each piece into a round bun, and place on a baking sheet covered with parchment paper, or lightly greased. Cover with a kitchen towel and let rise again about one hour.

Preheat oven to 400°F. Stir all the filling ingredients together well. After the rolls are ready for baking, take a flat-bottomed drinking glass about 2½ inches in diameter and press the bottom in the middle of the bun, spreading the bun out and forming a hollow in the middle. Mix the egg yolk with the milk and brush the edges with the glaze. Fill the middle with a full tablespoon of the cheese mixture, and bake the tarts for 15-20 minutes, or until nicely browned and the cheese filling is set.

BLUEBERRY PASTRY
Mustikkapiirakka

¼ pound butter (1 stick)
2 cups flour
¼ cup sugar
¼ teaspoon salt
2 envelopes dry yeast
¼ cup warm water
¼ cup cold milk
1 large egg

FILLING:
2 pints blueberries, washed and picked over
1 cup sugar
3 tablespoons potato starch or cornstarch
2 tablespoons fresh lemon juice

Blend the butter and the flour together until the mixture resembles coarse meal, add the sugar and salt and mix well. In a small bowl dissolve the yeast in the warm water, add the cold milk and the egg, and beat well together. Stir this into the flour mixture and knead lightly. If the dough is too sticky, add up to another ½ cup flour. Knead only lightly. You can also make this dough easily in a food processor, adding a little more flour if the machine begins to stall. Chill the dough for 20 minutes in the refrigerator. Take a piece of parchment paper, a little bigger than a jelly roll pan, and put it on a clean, dampened work surface. Roll the dough on the paper to a size about 1 inch larger than the jelly roll pan. Transfer the dough on the paper to the jelly roll pan, cover it lightly with a towel or plastic wrap, and let rise for about 1½ to 2 hours.

Preheat oven to 375°F and make the filling: In a saucepan mix the blueberries with the sugar, starch and lemon juice, and stir over medium heat until blueberries release some of their juices and the filling thickens. Spread the filling over the dough on the jelly roll pan, leaving a 1-inch margin all around. Fold the 1 inch of extra dough over the filling and pinch the corners. Bake the pastry for 20 minutes, or until edges are lightly browned and the filling bubbles. Let cool slightly and cut into 3-inch squares. Serve warm with ice cream or at room temperature with lightly whipped cream.

DANISH PASTRY
Wienerleivät

2 envelopes dry yeast
¼ cup warm water (110°F)
¾ cup milk
1 large egg, beaten
2 tablespoons sugar
½ teaspoon salt
1 teaspoon ground cardamom
1 tablespoon vegetable oil
3 cups flour
1 cup butter or margarine (2 sticks), slightly softened

GLAZE:
1 egg yolk

2 tablespoons milk

TOPPING:
½ cup powdered sugar
2 teaspoons water
Apricot or cherry preserves

In a 1 cup measuring glass dissolve the yeast in the warm water. Add cold milk to make 1 cup. In a mixing bowl combine the egg, milk, sugar, salt, cardamom and oil, mix in the flour, but do not knead. Refrigerate the dough for 15 minutes. On a well floured board knead the dough lightly and roll it into a square about ½-inch thick. Slice the butter on top of the dough making a square diagonally inside the dough. Bring the four corners of the dough to the center to form a "package" to hide the butter. Press the package carefully all over with the rolling pin and roll the dough into a rectangle. Fold the sides to the center and refrigerate for 15 minutes. Do the rolling and folding 2 more times, refrigerating the dough in between the rollings for 15 minutes. After the last rolling, refrigerate the dough again for 15 minutes.

To make the Danish, roll the dough into a square ½ inch thick, and cut it to ½-inch strips. Take the ends of the strips and twist them into ropes. Make a coil with the rope, bringing the end underneath. Alternately, you can cut the rolled dough into 4-inch squares and bring either the two opposing corners of the dough, or all four corners of the dough in the middle, forming a package. Press down firmly. Place a teaspoon of apricot jam in the middle of the pastry. Place them on a baking sheet covered with parchment paper or lightly greased, cover them loosely with plastic wrap and let rise in a cool place for an hour.

Preheat oven to 425°F. Mix one egg yolk with 2 tablespoons milk in a bowl, brush the pastries and sprinkle them with chopped nuts, if desired. Bake 10-15 minutes, or until nicely browned. Mix the powdered sugar with enough water to make a smooth icing. Put the icing into a plastic bag, cut a corner of the bag with scissors, and drizzle the icing over the Danish.

VIIPURI TWIST
Viipurin rinkeli

This is another Karelian specialty, named after the city of Viipuri which is now part of Russia. It is made of sweet bread dough that is flavored with nutmeg and cardamom and formed into a big round with ends twisted in the middle, rather like a pretzel.

3/4 cup milk
6 tablespoons butter or margarine
3/4 cup sugar
1 teaspoon ground cardamom
½ teaspoon ground nutmeg
½ teaspoon salt
¼ cup warm water (110°F)
1 envelope dry yeast
2 large eggs
3-3½ cups flour

GLAZE:
1 egg yolk
2 tablespoons milk

Heat the milk until small bubbles form on the side of the pan. Pour the milk into a large bowl and add the butter, sugar, cardamom, nutmeg and salt. Let cool until lukewarm. Dissolve the yeast in the warm water and add to the milk along with the lightly beaten eggs. Beat in 1½ cups of the flour and gradually stir in the rest of the flour. Knead the dough on a floured board until it is smooth and elastic. Place into a lightly oiled bowl, turn to coat the dough, cover with a kitchen towel and let rise in a warm place until double in bulk, about 1½ to 2 hours.

Turn the dough onto a floured board and knead until smooth. Divide the dough into two parts. Roll each part into a strand about 35-40 inches long, with about 8 inches of the ends thinner than the middle. Form each into a big circle, twisting the ends in the middle as in a pretzel and tucking the ends under the middle. Place on large baking sheets covered with parchment paper or lightly greased, cover with kitchen towels and let rise in a warm place for about an hour.

Preheat oven to 375°F. Mix the egg yolk with the milk, brush the twists with the mixture and bake for 20-25 minutes, or until golden brown. Cool on a rack, covered with kitchen towels.

Instead of making two big twists, you can divide the dough into smaller parts and make small twists. Baking time will be shorter, about 12-15 minutes.

CARDAMOM RUSKS
Korput

These are very popular in the summertime, as they keep well and can be transported easily to summer cottages and camping trips. They are perfect for dunking.

¾ cup milk
½ cup butter or margarine (1 stick)
1 envelope dry yeast
¼ cup warm water (110°F)
½ cup sugar
¼ teaspoon salt
1 teaspoon ground cardamom
1 large egg
3-3½ cups flour

GLAZE:
1 egg yolk
2 tablespoons milk

Heat the milk until small bubbles appear on the side of the saucepan, pour it into a large bowl, add the butter, cut into slices, and let cool to lukewarm. Dissolve the yeast in the warm water and add to the milk along with the sugar, salt, cardamom and egg. Add 1½ cups of the flour and beat for a few minutes with an electric mixer, until batter is smooth. Stir in more flour gradually, until the dough forms a ball. On a floured board knead the dough until it is smooth and elastic, adding just enough flour to make the dough clear the hands. Place the dough back in the bowl, cover with a kitchen towel, and let rise in a warm place for 1½-2 hours, or until double in bulk.

Punch the dough down, turn it onto a floured board, knead again and divide the dough in two. Form each part into a loaf and place them on a baking sheet covered with parchment paper, or lightly greased. Cover with a kitchen towel and let rise again for about 45 minutes.

Preheat oven to 375°F. Bake the loaves for 20-25 minutes until browned, and they sound hollow when tapped with a finger. Let cool, slice in 1-inch slices and cut each slice in half, lengthwise. Place the slices on a baking sheet and return them to oven for 10-15 minutes, until golden brown.

DOUGHNUTS
Munkit

3 tablespoons butter
3/4 cup milk
1 envelope dry yeast
¼ cup warm water (110°F)
1 egg
½ cup sugar
1 teaspoon ground cardamom
¼ teaspoon salt
2½-3 cups flour
Vegetable oil for frying

Melt the butter in a saucepan, add the milk and heat to lukewarm. Dissolve the yeast in the warm water. In a large bowl lightly beat the egg and sugar, and stir in the cardamom and salt. Add the milk mixture and the yeast and stir well. Beat in half the flour and gradually stir in enough flour for the dough to hold together. Knead until smooth, but do not add too much flour, the dough should be soft and sticky. Place the dough into a greased bowl, cover with a kitchen towel and let rise in a warm place for 1½-2 hours, or until double in bulk.

Punch the dough down, knead and divide it into 16 pieces. Roll these into small round buns. Cover with a kitchen towel and let rise in a warm place until double in bulk. Heat the oil in a fryer to 355-360°F. Oil that is too hot will brown them too quickly, before the dough inside is cooked. Fry them two or three at a time in the hot oil, turning once, until golden brown. Drain them on paper towels and roll on a plate filled with sugar before serving.

VIII.

CAKES AND COOKIES

LEMON CAKE
Sitruunakakku

3 large eggs
⅓ cup sugar
1 teaspoon finely grated fresh lemon peel
½ cup flour
1 teaspoon baking powder
½ cup powdered sugar
1 tablespoon fresh lemon juice

Preheat oven to 350°F. Butter and flour a 1½-quart loaf pan or decorative tube pan. Beat the eggs and the sugar until thick and lemon colored. Add the grated lemon peel. Sift the flour and the baking powder together and fold into the batter. Pour the batter carefully into the prepared pan. Bake for 20-30 minutes, or until a cake tester inserted in the middle comes out clean. Unmold on a rack. Mix the powdered sugar with the lemon juice and spoon over the cake. Let cool.

CREAM POUND CAKE
Savonlinnan kermakakku

1 cup heavy cream
1 teaspoon vanilla
2 large eggs
1 cup sugar
1½ cups flour
2 teaspoons baking powder

Preheat oven to 350°F. Butter and flour a 9-cup decorative tube pan or loaf pan. Whip the cream with the vanilla until thick. In another bowl beat the eggs and the sugar until thick and light colored, and fold into the cream. Sift the flour with the baking powder and fold into the mixture. Spoon the batter into the prepared pan and bake for about an hour, or until the cake is nicely browned and a cake tester inserted in the middle of the cake comes out clean. Cool 10 minutes before inverting the cake onto a wire rack to cool. Dust with powdered sugar before serving.

SAND CAKE
Hiekkakakku

1 cup butter or margarine (2 sticks)
1 cup sugar
3 large eggs
1 teaspoon vanilla
2 tablespoons brandy
1¼ cups flour
¾ cup potato starch or cornstarch
2 teaspoons baking powder

Preheat oven to 350°F. Butter and flour a 2-quart loaf pan or Bundt pan. Cream butter and half the sugar until light and fluffy. In another bowl beat the eggs with rest of the sugar, vanilla and brandy until thick and light colored. Combine the batters. Sift the flour together with the starch and the baking powder and fold well into the batter. Spoon the batter into the prepared pan and bake for about 40-50 minutes, or until cake tester inserted in the middle comes out clean. Unmold the cake onto a rack and when cool, dust with powdered sugar.

MARBLE CAKE
Tiikerikakku

1 cup butter or margarine (2 sticks)
1 cup sugar
3 large eggs
2 teaspoons vanilla
1½ cups flour

2 teaspoons baking powder
3 tablespoons cocoa powder
3 tablespoons milk

Preheat oven to 350°F. Butter and flour a 1½-quart decorative tube pan or loaf pan. Cream the butter and sugar until light and fluffy, add the eggs one by one, beating well after each addition, and beat in vanilla. In another bowl, mix the flour with the baking powder and add to the batter, beating until the flour is absorbed. Spoon 2/3 of the batter into the prepared pan. To the rest, add the cocoa powder and milk and beat until well mixed. Spread the cocoa mixture on top of the batter in the pan, and with a spatula cut and twist through the dough to get a marbled effect. Bake for about 50 minutes, or until a cake tester inserted in the middle comes out clean. Unmold on a rack to cool, and dust with powdered sugar before serving.

CARDAMOM CAKE
Kardemummakakku

½ cup butter or margarine (1 stick)
½ cup sugar
1 large egg
1¼ cups flour
1½ teaspoons baking powder
¼ teaspoon salt
1 teaspoon ground cardamom
½ cup milk

Preheat oven to 350°F. Butter and flour a 9-inch round cake pan, preferably one with a removable bottom. Cream the butter and sugar until fluffy, add the egg, and beat well. In a separate bowl, mix the flour, baking powder, salt and cardamom, and add gradually to the butter mixture, alternating with the milk. Spoon the batter into the prepared pan, and bake for about 30 minutes or until cake tester inserted in the middle comes out clean.

Remove the sides from the pan, let the cake cool, and cut in wedges to serve.

CURRANT CAKE
Korinttikakku

1 cup butter or margarine (2 sticks)
1 cup sugar
4 large eggs
2 teaspoons vanilla
1½ cups flour
2 teaspoons baking powder
4 ounces ground almonds (about ½ cup)
1 cup currants

Preheat oven to 350°F. Butter and flour a 2-quart loaf pan or Bundt pan. Cream the butter and the sugar until light and fluffy. Add the eggs one by one, beating well after each addition. Beat in the vanilla. In a separate bowl mix the flour, baking powder, ground almonds and currants and beat well into the batter. Spoon the batter into the prepared pan and bake for about 50 minutes, or until a cake tester inserted in the middle comes out clean. Unmold the cake on a rack and when cool, dust with powdered sugar.

LIGHT SPICE CAKE
Vaalea piparkakku

1¼ cups flour
1 teaspoon baking powder
2 teaspoons ground cardamom
2 teaspoons ground cinnamon
¼ teaspoon ground ginger
¼ teaspoon ground allspice
2 large eggs

1 cup sugar
½ cup half-and-half or milk
½ cup (1 stick) butter or margarine, melted

Preheat oven to 350°F. Butter and flour a 1½-quart decorative tube pan or loaf pan. Mix the spices and the baking powder into the flour. In another bowl, beat the sugar and eggs until thick and light colored. Stir in the flour mixture alternating with the half-and-half or milk, ending with the flour mixture. Fold in the melted butter last. Bake in the prepared pan for about 50 minutes, or until a cake tester inserted in the middle comes out clean. Unmold on a wire rack and when cool, dust with powdered sugar.

BUTTERMILK CAKE
Piimäkakku

This is a dark and moist spice cake, often served during Christmas season.

¾ cup buttermilk or plain yogurt
½ cup sugar
½ cup dark corn syrup or pancake syrup
1½ teaspoons ground cinnamon
½ teaspoon ground ginger
½ teaspoon ground cloves
½ teaspoon ground cardamom
¾ teaspoon baking soda
½ cup raisins
1¾ cups flour
⅓ cup melted margarine or vegetable oil

Preheat oven to 350°F. The dough will expand in the oven quite a bit, so select a 10-cup decorative Bundt pan or loaf pan. Butter and flour the pan. Mix all the ingredients together in the above order. Turn the dough into the prepared pan and bake for about 45 minutes, or until the cake starts shrinking from the sides of the pan and a cake tester inserted in the middle of the cake comes out clean. Let cool for 5 minutes before unmolding on a rack to cool.

DATE CAKE
Taatelikakku

This is not a cake for courting, but a rich holiday cake made with dates. It keeps very well and is best baked a week before you intend to use it. It also freezes very well.

1 package seedless dates (8 ounces), chopped
⅔ cup water
12 tablespoons (1½ sticks) butter or margarine
2 cups flour
2 teaspoons baking powder
1 teaspoon baking soda
2 large eggs
½ cup sugar
1 teaspoon vanilla
⅓ cup sour cream

In a saucepan simmer the dates in the water, covered, until soft, about 20 minutes. Remove from heat and add the butter or margarine, stirring occasionally until the butter has melted.

Preheat oven to 350°F. Butter and flour a 10-cup Bundt pan or loaf pan, since this cake will rise quite a bit in the oven. Sift together the flour with the baking powder and the baking soda. In another bowl, beat the eggs together with the sugar until well mixed, stir in the sour cream and the vanilla, add the flour mixture, and finally stir in the date and butter mixture. Pour the batter into the prepared pan and bake for 45-60 minutes, or until a cake tester inserted in the middle comes out clean. Unmold on a rack, let cool, wrap in plastic wrap and refrigerate a few days before serving.

POET'S CAKE
Runebergin kakku

This is a cake version of the popular pastries that are traditionally served on February 5th which is the birthday of Finland's national poet, J.L. Runeberg. There are several recipes for the pastries which are small straight-sided cupcakes, decorated with raspberry jam and sugar glaze. Instead of a cake, you can bake this dough in small muffin tins and get a close version of the original cakes. In that case you must reduce the baking time to 15-20 minutes.

12 tablespoons (1½ sticks) butter or margarine
3 large eggs
¾ cup sugar
1 cup cookie crumbs or graham cracker crumbs
1 cup ground almonds
¾ cup flour
1½ teaspoons baking powder
½ cup milk

FOR DECORATION:
½ cup powdered sugar
2 teaspoons cold water
Raspberry jam

Preheat oven to 325°F. Butter and flour a 9-inch round cake pan, preferably one with a removable bottom. Melt the butter and let cool. Beat the eggs and sugar until thick and pale yellow. In a separate bowl, mix the dry ingredients together and fold into the eggs. Fold in the melted butter and the milk. Turn the dough into the prepared cake pan and bake the cake for 45-50 minutes, or until a cake tester inserted in the middle comes out clean. Remove the cake from the pan and and slide it off the removable bottom, or turn it over with the help of a plate so that the baked side remains up. Let cool on a wire rack.

To decorate, mix the powdered sugar with a little bit of cold water to make a fairly thick paste. Spoon it into a heavy plastic food bag and snip a small hole in the corner of the bag with scissors. Squeezing the bag, decorate the cake with a diamond pattern, and drop a small amount of raspberry jelly in the center of each diamond. If you make cupcakes, make a circle in the center of the cupcake with the sugar glaze, and fill the middle with raspberry jelly.

JELLY ROLL
Kääretorttu

3 large eggs
½ cup sugar
1 teaspoon vanilla
4 tablespoons flour
2 tablespoons potato starch or cornstarch
1 teaspoon baking powder

FILLING:
1 cup of apricot, strawberry or raspberry jam, or applesauce, or fresh berries mashed with sugar to taste

Preheat oven to 375°F. Line a 10"x15" jelly roll pan with parchment paper, butter the paper and dust with flour. Beat the eggs with the sugar and the vanilla until thick and lemon colored. Mix the flour and the starch with the baking powder and sift over the eggs. Fold the flour well into the eggs and pour the dough in the prepared pan. Smooth it out evenly with a spatula. Bake in preheated oven for 7-10 minutes, or until the cake is lightly browned and springs back when pressed with a finger. Invert the cake on another sheet of parchment paper and peel the bottom paper off. Roll the cake from short end with the parchment paper into a roll and let cool. Unwrap the cake and spread with the filling. Roll the cake up again and cut the ends off. Place on a serving dish with the seam down, sprinkle with powdered sugar and serve in ½-inch slices.

CHOCOLATE ROLL
Unelmatorttu

3 large eggs
½ cup sugar
1 teaspoon vanilla
3 tablespoons potato starch or cornstarch
1 tablespoon flour
3 tablespoons cocoa powder
1 teaspoon baking powder

FILLING:
1½ cups powdered sugar
6 tablespoons butter, softened
2 tablespoons milk
½ teaspoon vanilla

Preheat oven to 375°F. Line a 10"x15" jelly roll pan with parchment paper, butter the paper and dust with flour. Beat the eggs with the sugar and vanilla until thick and lemon colored. Sift together the dry ingredients, and fold carefully into the batter. Spread the batter evenly on the pan and bake for 7-10 minutes, or until the cake springs back when touched with a finger. Invert the cake on another sheet of parchment paper and peel the bottom paper off. Roll the cake from the short end together with the parchment paper into a roll and let cool. When cool, unroll the cake, remove the paper, spread with the filling and roll the cake up again. Dust with powdered sugar before serving.

To make the filling: Beat the softened butter together with the powdered sugar, vanilla and milk to a smooth paste. Spread on the cake.

TOSCA CAKE
Toscakakku

2 large eggs
1 cup sugar
½ teaspoon almond extract
1 cup flour
1½ teaspoons baking powder
½ cup butter or margarine (1 stick), melted and cooled
¼ cup milk

Preheat oven to 325°F. Butter and flour a 9-inch round cake pan with removable bottom. Beat the eggs and sugar together until light and lemon colored. Beat in the almond extract. Sift the flour and the baking powder together and fold into the eggs, alternating with the melted butter and milk. Pour the batter into the prepared pan and bake for 30 minutes, or until a cake tester inserted in the middle of the cake comes out clean. Spread with the topping, increase the heat of the oven to 375°F and return the cake to the oven for 10 minutes, or until the topping is bubbling and golden brown. Do not let the topping burn.

TOPPING:
4 tablespoons butter or margarine
¼ cup sugar
1 tablespoon milk
1 tablespoon flour
¾ cup sliced almonds

In a saucepan melt the butter and add the sugar, milk, flour and sliced almonds. Mix well and cook stirring over medium heat until the mixture bubbles. Remove from heat.

CRANBERRY PIE
Karpalopiirakka

This pie is mostly made with lingonberries in Finland, but cranberries make a good substitute.

½ cup butter or margarine (1 stick)
¾ cup sugar
1 large egg
½ cup flour
⅔ cup whole wheat flour or rye flour

FILLING:
12-ounce package fresh cranberries, finely chopped
¾ cup sugar
1 large egg
1 cup sour cream
½ cup sugar
½ teaspoon vanilla

Preheat oven to 375°F. Cream butter and sugar until light and fluffy, beat in the egg and the combined flours. Press the dough into a buttered 9-inch pie plate with floured hands, spreading it up onto the sides of the pie plate.

Mix the chopped cranberries with ¾ cup sugar and spread over the dough on pie plate. Beat the egg together with the sour cream, ½ cup sugar and vanilla and pour over the cranberries. Bake for about 40 minutes, or until the filling is set and the crust browned at the edges. Serve chilled.

APPLE PIE
Omenapiiras

½ cup butter or margarine (1 stick)
½ cup sugar
1 large egg

1 cup flour
1 teaspoon baking powder

FILLING:
4-5 large Granny Smith or Golden Delicious apples, peeled, cored and thinly sliced
¼ cup sugar
½ teaspoon ground cinnamon

TOPPING:
4 tablespoons butter or margarine, softened
½ cup flour
¼ cup sugar
½ teaspoon ground cinnamon

Preheat oven to 350°F. Cream butter and sugar until light and fluffy, and beat in the egg. Sift together flour and baking powder, and beat into the mixture. Spread the dough with a spatula on a buttered 9-inch pie plate, making sure it covers the plate evenly, including the sides. Mix the apple slices with sugar and cinnamon, and spread evenly on the dough.

Mix the topping ingredients together until crumbly in texture, and sprinkle over the pie. Bake for about 40 minutes, or until the crumbs are browned. Test the apple filling with a fork to see if the apples are soft. If the apples need more cooking, cover the pie loosely with foil and cook the pie 5-10 minutes more.

STRAWBERRY CAKE
Mansikkakakku

2 large eggs
½ cup sugar
1 teaspoon vanilla
½ cup flour
1 teaspoon baking powder

FILLING:
1 pint strawberries
½ cup sugar

FROSTING:
1 cup heavy cream
2 tablespoons powdered sugar
1 teaspoon vanilla

Preheat oven to 350°F. Butter and flour a 9-inch round cake pan. Beat the eggs with the sugar and vanilla until thick and light. Sift the baking powder with the flour and fold into the eggs. Turn the batter into the prepared cake pan and bake for about 25 minutes or until cake tester inserted in the middle of the cake comes out clean. Invert the cake on a rack. When cool, slice carefully with a serrated knife into 3 layers.

Rinse and hull the berries. Set aside a few berries for decoration. With a fork mash the berries coarsely, and stir in the sugar. Layer the cake with the mashed strawberries. Whip the cream lightly with the powdered sugar and the vanilla and spread over the cake. Decorate with fresh strawberries. Refrigerate for an hour or two to allow the strawberry juices to moisten the cake.

CHOCOLATE CAKE
Suklaatorttu

2 eggs
½ cup sugar
1 teaspoon vanilla
6 tablespoons butter or margarine, melted
1 cup flour
2 tablespoons cocoa powder
1 teaspoon baking powder
¼ teaspoon baking soda
½ cup milk

CHOCOLATE FROSTING:

2 cups powdered sugar
4 teaspoons cocoa powder
2 tablespoons butter, melted
1 teaspoon vanilla
2 tablespoons hot water
¼ teaspoon instant coffee

TO DECORATE:

½ cup toasted almond slices or finely chopped walnuts

Preheat oven to 350°F. Beat the eggs with sugar until thick and light colored. Stir in vanilla and melted butter. Sift together the flour, cocoa powder, baking powder, and baking soda, and stir into the batter alternating with the milk. Butter and flour an 8-inch round cake pan and spoon in the batter. Bake for 25-30 minutes, or until a cake tester inserted in the middle comes out clean. Invert the cake on a rack and when cool, spread the top and sides with chocolate frosting. To decorate, press toasted almond slices or chopped walnuts to the sides of the cake with your hand.

To make the frosting, sift together the powdered sugar and cocoa in a bowl. Stir in the melted butter, vanilla and about 2 tablespoons hot water mixed with instant coffee. Keep stirring until the mixture reaches spreading consistency. If the mixture seems too thin, refrigerate for 15 minutes before spreading the frosting on top and sides of the cake.

FILLED DESSERT CAKE
Täytekakku

There isn't a feast in Finland that does not include one of these frosted and filled cakes. No matter what the filling is, the cake is always moistened with some kind of liquid and decorated, often with berries or fruits, and cream. This particular cake is a sampler, a spongecake filled with orange custard and decorated with fruits.

CAKE:

4 large eggs
1 cup sugar
2 teaspoons vanilla
2 teaspoons baking powder
1 cup flour

Preheat oven to 350°F. Butter and flour two 9-inch round cake pans. Beat the eggs and sugar until thick and lemon colored. Add the vanilla. Sift together the flour and the baking powder and fold into the batter. Spread the batter evenly between the two prepared pans and bake them for about 25 minutes, or until the cakes start shrinking from the edges and a cake tester inserted in the middle comes out clean. Let cool for a few minutes and invert the cakes on a rack to cool.

FILLING:

1½ tablespoons cornstarch
½ cup sugar
1 cup milk
2 large eggs
1 egg yolk
1 tablespoon orange-flavored liqueur
2 teaspoons vanilla

Mix all ingredients except the flavorings together in a saucepan. Place on medium heat and stir continuously with a wire whisk or a wooden spoon until the mixture thickens and becomes smooth and shiny. Remove from heat and stir in the liqueur and the vanilla. Let cool.

MOISTENING SYRUP:

½ cup water
¼ cup sugar
1 teaspoon orange-flavored liqueur

Bring the water to a boil, add the sugar and stir until the sugar has dissolved. Remove from heat and add the flavoring. Let cool.

FROSTING:

1 cup heavy cream
2 tablespoons powdered sugar
1 teaspoon vanilla
Sliced fruits, e.g., bananas, kiwis, peaches, strawberries

Whip the cream with powdered sugar and vanilla until thick, but not stiff. Set fruits aside.

GLAZE:

2 tablespoons apricot jam or red currant jelly
4 tablespoons water

Boil the apricot jam or red currant jelly with the water, stirring often, until thoroughly mixed and a drop from the stirring spoon clings a while before falling. If you use apricot jam, work through a sieve to remove the fruit particles.

ASSEMBLY:

With a serrated knife cut each cake in half horizontally. Place the first layer cut side up on a serving dish, moisten by sprinkling it with 2-3 tab lespoons of the syrup, and spread with 1/3 of the filling. Assemble the other layers the same way, always sprinkling the layers with the syrup. Place the top layer cut side down. After the top layer is in place, spread the top and sides with the whipped cream and place the fruits decoratively on the top. To prevent the fruits from drying out, spoon the glaze over them. Refrigerate the cake for an hour or two before serving.

MERINGUES
Marengit

4 egg whites
1 cup sugar

Preheat oven to 190°F. Beat the egg whites until soft peaks are formed when the beater is lifted. Gradually add sugar and keep beating until all sugar is added and the whites are glossy and very stiff. Fill a pastry bag with a star tip with the whites, or use a plastic bag and cut a small opening in one corner. Pipe the whites into small mounds about 1½ inches in diameter on a baking sheet lined with parchment paper or greased and dusted with flour. Bake for about 2 hours. Cookies should not brown, lower the heat if they start to turn color. After 2 hours turn the oven off, open the oven door and leave ajar, allowing the cookies to dry further until the oven cools. Store in an airtight tin.

AUNT HANNA'S COOKIES
Hanna-tädin kakut

These old-fashioned cookies have been baked in Finland for generations.

4 tablespoons butter
2/3 cup heavy cream
3/4 cup sugar
1 teaspoon vanilla
1¼ cup flour
3/4 cup potato starch or cornstarch
½ teaspoon baking soda

Preheat oven to 375°F. Melt the butter and let cool. Whip the cream with the sugar and the vanilla until just lightly whipped, not stiff. Add the melted butter. Sift together the flours and the baking soda and add to the mixture. It should be slightly sticky, but firm enough to handle. Roll small pieces of the dough into balls about an inch in diameter and set on a greased baking sheet or one lined with parchment paper, leaving a couple of inches between cakes to make room for expansion. Bake the cookies for about 10 minutes or until very lightly colored. Cool on a rack.

CINNAMON S-COOKIES
Kaneliässät

3 large eggs
1 cup sugar
½ cup butter or margarine (1 stick)
2½ cups flour
1 teaspoon baking powder
½ teaspoon ground cinnamon

TOPPING:
3 tablespoons sugar
1 teaspoon ground cinnamon

Beat the eggs with ½ cup of the sugar until thick and light. In another bowl, cream the butter with the rest of the sugar until fluffy. Sift together flour, baking powder and cinnamon. Fold all ingredients together and mix carefully until you get a fairly sticky dough. Chill for 10 minutes.

Preheat oven to 375°F. On a board roll pieces of the dough into strands the thickness of your little finger. Cut the strands into 3-inch pieces. Mix the sugar and the cinnamon on a plate and roll the pieces in the sugar, then bend them into S-shapes on a baking sheet lined with parchment paper or lightly greased. Bake the cookies for about 10 minutes or until very lightly browned.

RYE COOKIES
Ruiskakut

These cookies are made to resemble the sour rye loaves that are so popular in Finland. Finns will instantly recognize the shape.

1 cup butter or margarine (2 sticks)
½ cup sugar
1 cup rye flour
1 cup all-purpose flour
2 teaspoons baking powder
(1 tablespoon water)

Cream the butter and the sugar until light and fluffy. Sift the baking powder with the flours and stir into the butter. If the mixture is too crumbly to hold together, add the water and mix again. Chill the dough for 30 minutes.

Preheat oven to 375°F. Roll the dough quite thinly on a floured board. Cut out 3-inch circles with a cookie cutter and cut a hole in the center with a thimble or with the tip of a pastry bag. Prick all over with a fork. Place the cookies on a baking sheet covered with parchment paper, or lightly greased, and bake for 8-10 minutes, or until lightly browned. Cool on a rack.

SPOON COOKIES
Lusikkaleivät

½ pound butter (2 sticks)
¾ cup sugar
2 teaspoons vanilla
1¾-2 cups flour
¾ teaspoon baking soda
Raspberry or strawberry jam
Powdered sugar

In a saucepan melt the butter and let it brown lightly. Pour into a mixing bowl and add the sugar and the vanilla. Let cool.

Preheat oven to 325°F. Sift the flour and the baking soda together and stir into the butter mixture. The dough should be crumbly, but slightly sticky. Cover a baking sheet with parchment paper or grease it well. Take the dough by the teaspoonful, pressing it well down into the spoon, and invert it onto the baking sheet using your thumb. Form all the cookies this way. Bake them or 15 minutes, or until lightly browned. Cool. Spread some jam on the flat side of the cookie and cover with another cookie to make a sandwich. Dust with powdered sugar.

OATMEAL COOKIES
Kaurakeksit

1 cup butter or margarine (2 sticks)
1 cup sugar
1 cup flour
3 cups oatmeal
¾ teaspoon baking soda
½ cup heavy cream

Preheat oven to 375°F. Cream butter and sugar together until light and fluffy. In another bowl mix flour with oatmeal and baking soda and add to the butter mixture. Mix well. Add the heavy cream last by sprinkling it over the dough, and stir as little as possible to mix it in. With a teaspoon take small pieces of the dough and drop on a baking sheet that has been greased or lined with parchment paper. Leave a 2-inch space between the pieces, since the dough spreads out during baking. Bake for 10-12 minutes or until golden brown. Remove carefully with a spatula to cool on a rack.

COOKIE RUSKS
Pikkuleipäkorput

Rusks are very popular in Finland, especially during the summer, since they keep well. They are often made by cutting slices of pulla in half and drying the slices in the oven. This version is a little bit more like a cookie and is nice for dunking.

1 cup butter or margarine (2 sticks)
2 cups sugar
2 large eggs
5-5½ cups flour
4 teaspoons baking powder
1 teaspoon ground cardamom
1 cup milk

Preheat oven to 400°F. Cream the butter with the sugar until light and fluffy, add the eggs, one at a time, beating well after each addition. Sift the flour with the baking powder and the cardamom, and add, alternating with the milk, into the mixture, ending with the flour.

On a floured board, roll the dough half an inch thick and use a biscuit cutter to cut out round cakes about 2 inches in diameter. Place them onto a baking sheet that is greased or lined with parchment paper, and bake until lightly browned, about 11-13 minutes. Remove them from oven and let cool slightly, until you can handle them. With a fork split them in halves like English muffins, and place them again on the baking sheet with the split side up. Return them to oven and bake until lightly browned, about 8-10 minutes.

FORK COOKIES
Haarukkaleivät

12 tablespoons butter or margarine (1½ sticks)
⅓ cup sugar

1 large egg
2 teaspoons vanilla
1⅓ cups flour
1 teaspoon baking powder
3 tablespoons cocoa

Cream the butter and sugar until light and fluffy. Add the egg and vanilla and beat well. Sift the flour, baking powder and cocoa together and add to the butter mixture. Dough will be very soft. Chill for 30 minutes.

Preheat oven to 375°F. Roll the dough between hands into balls about 1 inch in diameter. Place them on a baking sheet lined with parchment paper or greased lightly. Flatten the balls with a fork by pressing crosswise markings on the cookies. To prevent sticking, dip the fork in cold water between cookies. Bake for 10-15 minutes, or until lightly browned.

MANOR HOUSE COOKIES
Herrasväenleivät

1 cup butter (2 sticks)
½ cup sugar
1½ cups flour
½ cup potato starch or cornstarch
Raspberry jam

Cream the butter and the sugar together until light and fluffy. Mix the flour and the starch together and beat into the dough. Chill for 20 minutes in the refrigerator.

Preheat oven to 350°F. On a well floured board roll the dough about ¼ inch thick and with a cookie cutter cut rounds about 2 inches in diameter. Place the rounds on a baking sheet lined with parchment paper, or lightly greased, and bake the cookies for about 10-15 minutes, or until lightly browned. Cool cookies on a rack, and when cool, carefully press two cookies together with ½ teaspoon of raspberry jam in between.

BUTTER COOKIES
Murokakut

1 cup butter (2 sticks)
1 cup sugar
1 large egg
½ teaspoon almond extract
1 teaspoon baking powder
1¾ cups flour

Cream the butter and sugar together until light and fluffy, add the egg and almond extract and beat well. Mix the baking powder and flour together and add to the dough, mixing well. Chill for 20 minutes.

Preheat oven to 400°F. Place the dough into a pastry bag fitted with a small star tip. Pipe the dough onto an ungreased baking sheet into small circles about 2 inches in diameter. Bake for 10 to 12 minutes, until light brown.

ALEXANDER'S TARTS
Aleksanterintortut

When Finland was a Grand Duchy of Russia, and Czar Alexander II was Governor General of Finland, many advances were made to secure rights to the Finnish nation. One of them was the use of Finnish language in schools and offices, along with Swedish that had been used ever since Finland was part of Sweden. Another one was the creation of a new monetary unit, the markka. In gratitude the Finns named a street in central Helsinki after the Czar (Aleksanterinkatu), erected a statue for him in the Senate Square and named these little tarts Alexander's tarts.

1 cup butter (2 sticks)
½ cup sugar
1 large egg
2 cups flour

FILLING:
½ cup raspberry jam

ICING:
1¼ cups powdered sugar
4-5 teaspoons hot water
¼ teaspoon almond extract
Red food coloring

Preheat oven to 400°F. Cream butter and sugar together until light and fluffy, beat in the egg, stir in the flour and mix until the dough can be formed into a ball. Avoid overmixing. Chill for 30 minutes. Cut two sheets of parchment paper the size of a baking sheet. Cut the dough in half. Place the parchment paper on a dampened work surface and on it roll one part of the dough into a thin rectangle. Lift the parchment paper with the dough on it onto a baking sheet and bake for about 10 minutes, or until lightly browned. Do the same with the other part of the dough, trying to shape both rectangles the same size. Remove from oven, slide the parchment paper with dough on an even surface and let cool slightly. Spread the raspberry jam evenly over one cake and carefully slide the other sheet of the cake off parchment paper and on top. Press lightly together.

In a small bowl mix the powdered sugar with the water and the almond extract until spreadable. Mix about 1 teaspoon of water with a drop of red food coloring and add enough to sugar to make light pink. Mix well. Spread this over the doubled-up cake and with a sharp knife cut into 2"x3" rectangles. Wait until the icing is dry, and loosen the tarts onto a serving dish.

SPICE COOKIES
Piparkakut

These cookies are on every table in Finland during the Christmas season. There are several recipes for these, this particular one being very delicate and crumbly. This dough cannot be used for baking cookie houses, as these cookies are too delicate.

1 cup (2 sticks) butter
1 large egg
1 cup sugar
1 tablespoon dark corn syrup or pancake syrup
1 teaspoon baking soda
2 teaspoons ground cardamom
1 teaspoon ground cinnamon
½ teaspoon ground ginger
½ teaspoon ground cloves
2½-3 cups flour

Melt the butter in a saucepan and let cool. In a mixing bowl beat the egg, sugar, syrup, baking soda and spices. Add the melted butter and mix well. Mix in the flour and gather the dough into a ball. Refrigerate for 24 hours.

Preheat oven to 375°F. Roll the dough into a fairly thin layer on a floured board and with cookie cutters take out small cakes. Set them on a baking sheet covered with parchment paper or lightly greased, and bake for about 5 minutes, or until lightly browned.

Instead of refrigerating the dough in one piece, you can work the dough into rolls a couple of inches thick, wrap them in foil and refrigerate. The next day remove the foil, slice the dough into thin round cakes and bake as directed.

RAUMA COOKIES
Rauman piparkakut

Rauma is a charming small town on the coast of western Finland, the third oldest in Finland and well over 500 years old. It is famous for its delicate handmade laces, and for the well-preserved old wooden buildings in the town center which is on the United Nations list of world heritage sites. Obviously, Rauma has good bakers as well.

2 large eggs
1¼ cups dark brown sugar
½ cup (1 stick) butter or margarine, melted
½ cup sour cream
1 tablespoon brandy
2 cups flour
¾ cup cookie crumbs or graham cracker crumbs, sifted
1 teaspoon baking soda
3 teaspoons baking powder
½ teaspoon ground cinnamon
½ teaspoon ground cloves
½ teaspoon ground cardamom
½ teaspoon ground mace or nutmeg

Beat the eggs with the sugar in a mixing bowl until light. Stir in the melted butter, sour cream and brandy. In another bowl, sift together the flour, bread crumbs, soda, baking powder and spices, and stir the flour mixture into the egg mixture. Mix well. Dough will be very soft. Refrigerate overnight.

Preheat oven to 350°F. Roll the dough between palms of hands into balls about 1 inch in diameter and place them on a cookie sheet lined with parchment paper, or lightly greased. Bake until nicely browned, about 15 minutes. Let cookies dry at room temperature a day before storing them in airtight tins.

CHRISTMAS PRUNE TARTS
Joulutortut

These pastries are a must at Christmastime. You can buy them in all the bakeries during December, but a lot of families make them at home. The pastries freeze well and profit from warming them lightly before serving. The cheese used in the Finnish dough is the kind that is not available here, rahka, but cream cheese or ricotta cheese are acceptable substitutes. The tarts can also be made with ordinary pie dough or puff pastry dough, which is often used in store-bought prune tarts.

FILLING:

12-ounce package pitted prunes
½ cup sugar
¼ teaspoon vanilla

Prepare filling first: In a saucepan cook the prunes in water to cover for about 20 minutes. Drain and reserve the liquid. Place the fruit and sugar in a food processor or blender with ¼ cup of the liquid. Process until smooth, adding a little more liquid if necessary. Return the mixture to a saucepan and stir it over heat until mixture comes to a boil and thickens. Remove from heat, stir in the vanilla and let cool.

PASTRY:

1 cup butter or margarine (2 sticks)
2½ cups flour
8 ounces cream cheese or ricotta cheese

To make pastry: Blend the butter and flour together until mixture resembles coarse meal. Add the cheese and mix until the dough forms a ball. This is easily done in a food processor. Wrap and chill the dough for 30 minutes.

Preheat oven to 375°F. Divide the dough in two parts. Roll out the dough, one part at a time, on a floured board to a thin sheet. With a cookie cutter or a wide drinking glass cut out rounds of about 3½ inches in diameter. Put a teaspoon of filling in the center of each round, brush the edges with water and fold over to make a half moon. Press the edges together and crimp with a fork. Bake the tarts for about 20 minutes or until lightly browned. Dust with powdered sugar before serving.

CHRISTMAS PINWHEEL TARTS
Joulutorttutähdet

This is another version of Christmas prune tarts, made with puff pastry. Instead of making your own dough, you may use frozen puff pastry sheets available in most supermarkets.

2 cups flour
½ teaspoon salt
Cold water
1 cup butter or margarine (2 sticks)
2 tablespoons sugar
10 cooked or ready to eat prunes, pitted and halved, or ½ cup prune filling, (page 214)

Mix flour, salt and about 3/4 cups cold water until you get a smooth dough. Wrap and chill for 20 minutes.

On a floured board roll the dough into a thin 12-inch square. Slice the butter and arrange the slices into a smaller square diagonally inside the dough. Fold the corners over the butter to make a "package." Roll the "package" carefully with a rolling pin into a rectangle and fold it in three. Wrap and chill 15 minutes. Roll and fold the dough 4-5 times, chilling it between every rolling.

Preheat oven to 400°F. Divide the dough in two equal pieces, and roll each into a thin square. Sprinkle each with one tablespoon sugar. With a pastry cutter divide the dough into 3½-inch squares. Make one-inch diagonal cut toward center from each corner of each square. Bring alternate corners together in the middle to form a pinwheel and press down firmly. Place a piece of prune or 1 teaspoon prune filling in the center and bake the pastries in oven for about 15-20 minutes, or until lightly browned. These pastries are best warmed-up before serving.

MAY DAY CRULLERS
Tippaleivät

These are served on May Day festivities with the sparkling May Day drink, sima. They are sold in all bakeries and coffee shops around that time, but are easy to make at home, too.

1 large egg
¼ cup sugar
¼ teaspoon salt
⅔ cup milk
1 cup flour
1 teaspoon baking powder
Hot oil for frying
Powdered sugar

Beat the egg lightly with sugar, add the salt and the milk. Sift the flour with the baking powder and beat into the eggs until smooth. Pour the dough into a strong plastic bag and cut a ¼-inch opening to one corner of the bag with scissors. Twist the bag closed and drizzle the dough into the hot (375°F) oil and try to form small birds nests, two or three at a time. When brown on the underside, turn them over. When brown on both sides, remove and drain on paper towels. Before serving, sprinkle with powdered sugar.

IX.
DRINKS

GLOGG
Glögi

1 cup water
1 cup sugar
10 whole cloves
½ teaspoon whole cardamom seeds from cardamom pods
2 cinnamon sticks
1 slice of orange peel, cut from an orange with a vegetable peeler
1 bottle red wine
1 bottle port
1 cup raisins
1 cup blanched almonds
(1 cup brandy)

Simmer the water with the sugar and the spices, covered, for 15 minutes. Strain the spices out of the water, add the wine and the port along with the raisins and almonds, and heat, but do not boil. Just before serving add the brandy. Serve in small cups with a few raisins and almonds in each cup.

FRUIT JUICE GLOGG
Mehuglögi

2 cups water
3 tablespoons sugar
12 whole cloves
2 cinnamon sticks
½ teaspoon cardamom seeds from cardamom pods or ¼ teaspoon ground cardamom
1 cup grape juice
1 cup apple juice
(2 tablespoons raisins)
(2 tablespoons blanched almonds)

Simmer the water with the sugar, cloves, cardamom and cinnamon, covered, for 15 minutes. Strain the spices out of the water and add the juices, and if desired, the raisins and the almonds. Heat and serve hot in mugs, with a few raisins and almonds in every mug.

LEMON-FLAVORED MEAD
Sima

This is the drink that is customarily served on May Day. It is still often homemade, although soft drink manufacturers prepare and bottle it just for the occasion.

8 cups water
1 lemon
1 cup sugar
⅓ cup dark brown sugar
⅛ teaspoon dry yeast
A few raisins

Wash the lemon well and peel the yellow zest off with a potato peeler. Save the zest and squeeze the lemon to extract the juice. Bring 4 cups of water to boil in a 3-quart stainless steel or enameled saucepan. Stir in the sugars and remove the pan from the heat. Add 4 cups cold water, the lemon juice and the zest pieces. Let the drink cool to lukewarm. Take a couple of tablespoonfuls of the liquid and dissolve the yeast in it. Stir the yeast into the liquid, cover the pan and let the liquid stay at room temperature overnight.

When the liquid starts to ferment (small bubbles start to form and the lemon peels rise to the surface), pour it into clean bottles. Add 1 teaspoon sugar and a few raisins into each bottle, close them tightly and refrigerate. In a couple of days the raisins will rise to the surface and the drink is ready. Remove the raisins and serve ice cold. If you double the recipe, don't double the amount of yeast, it will ferment even a larger amount of liquid.

STRAWBERRY MILK
Mansikkamaito

The drink may also be made with blueberries.

1 pint halved strawberries
2 cups milk
2 tablespoons sugar
2 ice cubes

Combine all ingredients in a blender and blend until smooth. Serve immediately. Serves 3.

X.

PORRIDGES AND MILK SOUPS

Finns have always eaten a lot of grain. In addition to a multitude of breads, Finns cook the grain or flour in water or milk to make breakfast cereals, snacks and desserts. Porridges are made with oatmeal, rye flour, rice, barley, farina, buckwheat and millet. Another very popular dish is grain or flour cooked in milk to make a loose porridge, called velli. The English word for it is "gruel", but the dish is just too delicious to be saddled with such a name. That is why I have called them milk soups. They make a nice breakfast on a cold morning, or a nutritious snack. In earlier times, some college students were known to live on a diet of porridges, since they are inexpensive, nutritious and filling. Porridges and soups made with milk are easiest to cook in a double boiler, to prevent scorching.

OATMEAL PORRIDGE
Kaurapuuro

4 cups water or milk
1½ cups oatmeal
½ teaspoon salt

Heat the water or milk in a nonstick saucepan. Stir in the oatmeal, reduce heat and let simmer for 10-20 minutes, stirring often. Add the salt. Serve with milk and sugar, or with a pat of butter and milk.

MILK SOUP WITH OATMEAL
Kauravelli

4 cups milk
⅓ cup oatmeal
½ teaspoon salt

Heat the milk in a nonstick saucepan and stir in the oatmeal.

Reduce heat and simmer for 10-20 minutes, stirring often. Add salt and serve, sprinkled with sugar, if desired.

RYE PORRIDGE
Ruispuuro

4 cups water
1 cup rye flour
½ teaspoon salt

Bring the water to boil. Sprinkle in the salt and the rye flour while beating with a wire whisk. Stir with a wooden spoon until the porridge thickens. Let simmer over very low heat, stirring often, for 1 hour. Serve with a pat of butter and milk.

MILK SOUP WITH FARINA
Mannavelli

4 cups milk
¼ cup farina
½ teaspoon salt

In a double boiler over simmering water bring the milk to boil. Sprinkle in the farina and keep stirring until the soup thickens slightly. Let cook for about 30 minutes, stirring occasionally. Add salt. Serve sprinkled with sugar and cinnamon, if desired.

BARLEY PORRIDGE
Ohrapuuro

1 cup boiling water
½ cup barley
4 cups milk
¾ teaspoon salt

On top of a double boiler over simmering water mix the barley with the hot water. Cover and let cook until the water is absorbed. Stir in the milk and let cook covered, stirring occasionally. Barley porridge takes a long time to cook: pearled barley about 2-3 hours, whole barley about 4-5 hours. The porridge should thicken, the grains should be very soft, and the dish should look slightly pink. When the porridge is done, stir in the salt and serve with milk and sprinkled with sugar, and cinnamon, if desired.

MILK SOUP WITH BARLEY
Ohravelli

⅓ cup barley
1 cup boiling water
4 cups milk
¾ teaspoon salt
(1 teaspoon potato starch or cornstarch)

In a double boiler over simmering water, mix the barley with the hot water, cover and cook until the water is absorbed. Add the milk, and cook the soup over barely simmering water until it thickens and the barley is tender, about 4-5 hours. A properly cooked barley soup looks slightly pink. For slightly thicker soup, mix 1 teaspoon of potato starch or cornstarch with a little bit of cold water and stir into the soup. When the soup is done, stir in the salt, and serve in big soup plates, sprinkled with sugar.

MILK SOUP WITH MACARONI
Makaronivelli

¾ cup elbow macaroni
3 cups milk
1 tablespoon cornstarch
¼ cup water

½ teaspoon salt
1 teaspoon sugar

Boil macaroni according to package directions and drain. Bring milk to boil in a nonstick saucepan, add the drained macaroni and simmer for a few minutes, stirring. Mix the cornstarch with the water and beat into the soup. Let simmer for a few minutes more while stirring. Add the salt and sugar, and serve.

MILK SOUP WITH RICE
Riisivelli

½ cup rice
1 cup water
4 cups milk
Cinnamon stick
½ teaspoon salt
(1 teaspoon potato starch or cornstarch)

In a double boiler on top of simmering water bring the rice and water to boil, cover and cook until the water is absorbed, about 15 minutes. Add the milk and cinnamon stick and cook over simmering water, stirring occasionally, for about an hour. If you like a thicker soup, mix the potato starch or cornstarch with a little bit of cold water and stir into the soup. Remove the cinnamon stick and stir in the salt. Serve in big soup plates, sprinkled with sugar.

RICE AND APPLE PORRIDGE
Herkkupuuro

3 cups peeled, cored and chopped apples
4 cups water
⅔ cup rice
Cinnamon stick

¼ cup sugar
⅛ teaspoon salt

Bring the water to boil and add the chopped apples, the rice and the cinnamon stick. Let simmer, stirring occasionally, about 30 minutes. Remove the cinnamon stick and stir in the salt and sugar. Serve with cream or milk.

METRIC CONVERSION TABLE

VOLUME MEASURES

American	Metric
1 cup = 8 fluid ounces	2.37 deciliters (dl)
1 pint = 2 cups	4.74 deciliters
1 quart = 4 cups	9.46 deciliters
1 tablespoon	1.5 centiliters (cl)
1 teaspoon	0.5 centiliters
½ cup minus 1 tablespoon	1 deciliter
⅔ cup	1.5 deciliters (Scandinavian coffee cup)
1 quart plus ¼ cup	1 litre

WEIGHT MEASURES

American	Metric
1 pound = 16 ounces	453 grams
1 ounce	28 grams
3½ ounces	100 grams
2.2 pounds	1000 grams = 1 kilogram

OVEN TEMPERATURES

160°F	71°C
170°F	77°C
200°F	93°C
225°F	107°C
250°F	121°C
275°F	135°C
302°F	150°C
325°F	163°C
350°F	177°C
375°F	190°C
400°F	205°C
425°F	218°C
450°F	232°C
475°F	246°C
500°F	260°C

MAIL-ORDER SOURCES

Crate and Barrel
725 Landwehr Road
Northbrook, IL 60062
Tel. 1-800-323-5461
Cookware, glassware, dinnerware
Catalog (free)

Erickson's Delicatessen
5250 N. Clark Street
Chicago, Illinois 60640
Tel. 312-561-5634
Scandinavian foods
Catalog (free)

Finnart
2543 Lariat Lane
Walnut Creek CA 94596-6600
Tel. 510-935-6375
Finnish giftware, dinnerware
Catalog ($3)

Glada Grisen
905 Main Street
Lake Geneva, WI 53147
Tel. 1-800-688-0905
Finnish books, music, giftware, some foods
Catalog (free)

Ingebretsen's Scandinavian Center
1601 E. Lake Street
Minneapolis, MN 55407
Tel. 1-800-279-9333
Cookware, giftware, foods
Catalog (free)

Anderson Butik
P.O. Box 151
Lindsborg, Kansas 67456
Tel. 1-800-782-4132
Giftware, foods
Catalog ($2, refundable)

The Finlanders
Box 418
Owen, Wisconsin 54460
Tel. 715-229-4314
Finnish giftware, linens
Catalog (free)

INDEX